GIRLS' LIFE MAGAZINE

GL The Girls' Life Guide to Being the Best You!

Edited by
Kelly White

Illustrated by
Lisa Parett

Scholastic Inc.

New York • Toronto • London • Auckland • Sydney
Mexico City • New Delhi • Hong Kong • Buenos Aires

ISBN: 0-439-44978-2

Copyright © 2003 by Girls' Life Magazine.

Design: Mark Neston

12 11 10 9 8 7 6 5 4 3 2 1   3 4 5 6 7 8/0

Printed in the U.S.A.

First Scholastic printing, April 2003

Contents

Just Saying Hi!

The thing about striving to be your absolute best is that you don't have to morph your whole persona. You're already incredible, amazing, and fabulous! Being your best self is about taking a good look at yours truly and becoming aware of your most awesome qualities. And being your best self begins with self-esteem. Without positive self-esteem, you can't work those fantastic qualities you're packing to your full advantage. In this book, we'll help you bring it up a notch (maybe more)!

We'll tell you what self-esteem is, why it's important, and how to make it work for you. What you probably don't realize is how many facets of your life are tied to your self-esteem. One of the biggies is your body image. We'll show you a whole new way of looking at that beautiful bod you were blessed with—so you can learn to truly like your reflection in the mirror!

And because school is such a huge part of your world, it's important to get in touch with your inner star student. We'll help you work what strenghs you have—all while spelunking your way through the academic stuff that makes school such a challenge.

Don't think for a second we've overlooked all the other challenges life throws your way. When you have a strong sense of self, things like nasty gossip, lies, and trying to live up to impossible ideals can all be dealt with, head on.

Last but not least, muster up some spunk, shake your shy-bee ways, and come face to face with your fears so you can continue to become more and more sure of true-blue, fabulous you!

Karen

Karen Bokram
Editor-in-Chief, *GL*

1

Step Up to Super Self-Esteem

Step Up to Super Self-Esteem

Here's a question for you: How do you *really* feel about the most important person in your life? Think about it...think hard. Stumped? Maybe that's because you're thinking of your fuzzy feelings for your mom or grandparent or best bud. Those people are great, but in case you haven't figured it out yet, the most important person in your life is *you*! That's why it's so crucial to be in touch with your "I like myself" factor— and that takes a certain self-awareness.

EXTREME SELF-ESTEEM!

Self-esteem. You've probably heard that phrase a lot. But just in case you aren't sure what it means, we'll save you a trip to the dictionary. Self-esteem is how you feel about yourself. If you believe in yourself, and know you're smart or fun or nice or talented (or all of the above), that means your self-esteem pretty much rocks.

Why is it such a big deal to have good self-esteem? Well, for starters, girls with high self-esteem feel confident, competent, and valued. In other words, they like themselves. Girls with low self-esteem commonly have feelings of insecurity and self-doubt. If that's the case, you have the girl power to turn your self-esteem around....

5

Your Self-Esteem in Action

Self-esteem affects your whole world—every conversation, relationship, and decision. If you feel good about yourself, you're more likely to talk to a teacher about an unfair grade or go out for softball tryouts. If you aren't so sure of yourself, chances are you'll let friends decide your weekend plans for you or cop out before you've even given violin lessons a fair shot.

What shapes your self-esteem? Self-esteem is affected by lots of things—how you've been treated, what goals you've achieved, failures you've overcome. To understand the impact self-esteem has, read about three girls: Nicole, Ann, and Kelly. You'll see how each girl's self-esteem was shaped by her experiences...and what each has done about it.

Nicole's Story

Nicole and her BFF, Jen, used to do everything together. They were stuck together like glue. But suddenly Jen was spending less and less time with Nicole, and Nicole felt alone and out of place. She had always thought that her friendship with Jen would last forever. "How was I supposed to know she'd become instant BFFs with a girl on her basketball team and cut me out?" she asks. Nicole tried to win Jen back, but it was hopeless.

Everybody else seemed so involved with their own friends that Nicole, who hadn't had to make new friends for a long time, was uneasy. She was afraid to jump in on conversations. It wasn't long before she was complaining to her mother that the kids in school were selfish and unfriendly—nobody asked her to eat lunch with them or to study together.

Nicole's outlook finally turned around after her parents attended the school's open house. Nicole's English teacher told them Nicole was quiet in class. She said that whenever she asked Nicole a question, Nicole looked down and murmured, and it had gotten worse as weeks went on. When Nicole's parents reported this back to her, Nicole was surprised and said, "I've never been quiet in my life!" In class, she began paying more attention—to herself—and realized her teacher was right. "No wonder kids didn't want to talk to me," says Nicole. "I never put myself out there."

So Nicole made a conscious effort to snap out of it. She spoke up more in class and at lunch, joining conversations with girls she'd never talked to before. "At first, it was terrifying,"

she says. "I was so worried people would ignore me when I opened my mouth. But I figured it wouldn't be any worse than sitting there like a statue. When they answered me, it was such a relief."

It was no piece of cake, but making friends got a lot easier. Nicole realized her negative feelings about herself had made it hard for her to make new friends. "I had convinced myself that since my best friend dumped me, something must be wrong with me," she says. "So I gave up. I didn't realize *I* was the one who wasn't friendly. That's why no one wanted to get to know me!"

Nicole had fallen into a common self-esteem trap: Once she decided something was wrong with her, she believed it and acted as if it were true. This made her seem shy and unapproachable—and people responded accordingly. Nicole took advantage of her teacher's feedback to look at herself in a new way. Now Nicole is having a blast bonding with her new buds. She's never had so much fun—not even with Jen.

Ann's Story

Ann has been a competitive swimmer since she was six years old. Her parents were always majorly involved with her swimming, too—attending all her meets and practices,

discussing her progress with her coaches, and reminding her of what she needed to work on. Ann always appreciated her parents' interest, but she started feeling pressured, and soon the butterflies she'd get before meets turned into full-blown stomachaches. "I hated that look of disappointment on my parents' faces when I didn't win a race," she says.

Ann began to dread her swim meets. She soon hated practices, and her schoolwork suffered, too. "I had to give a timed oral report in English," she says. "As soon as I saw the teacher take out a stopwatch, I felt sick. The watch was just to make sure we didn't speak for more than four minutes, but I felt, like with swimming, that I was being measured to the 100th of a second."

The last straw came when Ann asked her parents if she could skip a swim meet and go to a slumber party—they didn't go for it. They said she needed to win the upcoming race in order to qualify for a later competition. Ann blew up. "It's my friend's birthday!" she yelled. "Maybe this party is more important to me than a stupid swim meet!"

"It hit me that I was only swimming to please them," Ann says, "and it took the fun out of it." She realized then that she wanted to stop competing. When she told her parents, they said she shouldn't be a quitter. But when she told her coach, he asked if Ann would instead help teach swimming to some physically challenged kids. Ann figured it was worth a try. And she loved it!

Afraid of their disapproval, Ann put off telling her parents. Slowly, she gathered her courage and took the straight route. "I've decided to do volunteer work instead of competing," she told them. "Teaching these kids makes me feel great." Ann's parents weren't thrilled, but they accepted it.

Recently, Ann decided to return to racing—on her own terms. She joined a local swim team that is laid back and not so competitive. After this experience, she feels able to be more direct in expressing her feelings: "I don't always get what I want, but at least I can ask now." It took a lot of courage, but by recognizing her needs and talents, doing what gives her satisfaction, speaking up for herself, and resolving a conflict with her parents, Ann's self-esteem has soared.

School has always been Kelly's thing. She loves reading and writing creative stories, and has a knack for remembering details. Her mom and dad are big on education. "You must be proud of yourself," they'd say whenever she got good grades on a report card. And Kelly was.

So, it came as a total shock when she failed a quiz for the first time. Since it was her first geography quiz, she'd had no idea what to expect. "I studied," she says, "but I'd go blank when I saw a map. I was clueless." She'd fill in what she could, knowing she was blowing it.

When her teacher returned the quizzes and Kelly saw she'd gotten a 58%, she got very upset. She'd never felt so dumb. She couldn't stop thinking about what her parents would say about the grade. That night, when she finally told them, she was surprised to find they weren't angry at all.

On the next round of quizzes, Kelly scored a 75%. After all the extra studying she had done, she was devastated. Her parents tried to help Kelly figure out why she was having such a tough time. "I just can't do it," she told them. They told her that geography tests call for some new study methods.

But whatever Kelly tried, it didn't work in time for the third quiz. She was stumped again and, for the first time ever, she tried to peek at someone else's answers. Finally, she gave up and handed in the quiz unfinished. "I knew I'd hit a low point," Kelly confides. "I certainly wasn't used to cheating. I was obviously losing it."

Hitting this low helped Kelly return to her senses. She decided to beat her problem, fair and square. First, she bought a computer geography game that her mom recommended, and she practiced filling in blank maps her dad designed for her. Slowly, her grade went up. "I had to change my expectations," she admits. "I would have loved a 95%, but when I got an 80%, it was a huge improvement...and a relief."

Kelly didn't let her struggle bring down the rest of her world, and she learned a lot about herself. Sure, failing a quiz took her by surprise, so she felt shaken up at first. But, she asked for help and tackled the problem. No one is immune to periods of self-doubt, but if you make the best of them and get the support you need, your self-esteem will be stronger in the long run.

Raising Your Self-Esteem

Nicole, Ann and Kelly each had their own hurdles to clear, but they all learned important lessons about what can screw up self-esteem—and what can boost it. Could your own self-esteem use a little jump start? Here are some secrets to help kick it up a notch.

✿ *Get to know yourself better.* Figure out your real thoughts, feelings, and needs. Ask yourself, "What do I value about myself?" and "What is important to me?" Determine your coolest qualities, and appreciate them. Recognize that you're honest, compassionate, kind, funny, athletic, artistic, smart, or whatever you are. You're fab, so feel it!

✿ *Remain true to your values.* There will be times when you might consider crossing a line, whether it's by cheating, lying, or doing something else you know is a definite no-no. During those times, remind yourself that there are *always* other options. You never have to do something that goes against the stellar standards you've set for yourself. Work on choosing activities and making choices that fit in with who you are, or who you want to be.

✿ *Know your strengths.* Discovering your interests and talents is totally important. But accept your limitations, too. You don't have to be the star of the stage or ace every test to feel proud. Some girls feel great about getting along with a sister or making it to the bus stop on time. Others feel good about helping with dinner or wearing their retainers for two nights in a row. Set realistic goals, and work on achieving them. If you don't succeed at first, don't give up—rethink your strategy. And be sure to congratulate yourself for every achievement.

✿ **Talk to yourself.** What you say to yourself is a huge part of self-esteem. Yes, there will always be people who don't like you, and situations you can't change. You don't usually have control over this. But you *do* have control over what you tell yourself. Whether you interpret situations positively or negatively is up to you. When you're in a bad mood, it's easy to think the worst and to talk yourself into thinking you're no good. But, think positive. Forget, "I must be a jerk if she doesn't want to be my friend anymore!" Try, "Her loss. It's time to make new friends." Remember past accomplishments, and tell yourself, "I can do this!"

✿ **Add it up.** Understand that self-esteem has its ups and downs. You can't expect to feel wonderful about yourself *all* the time. All that matters is that when you tally up your plusses and minuses, the total sum is a positive number. And that, girl, is extreme self-esteem!

BE YOUR OWN CHEERLEADING SQUAD— LEARN TO LOVE YOURSELF

Congratulations! You now know some secrets to raising your self-esteem. Now you need to learn how to keep those confident thoughts and feelings cranking. So what's the biggest self-esteem zapper? Self-doubt.

You know those cartoons where a devil sits on someone's shoulder whispering mischief in one ear, while an angel sits on the opposite shoulder advising the person to ignore the little red troublemaker? Think of self-doubt as that devil, saying stuff that undermines your self-esteem. Ever find yourself thinking stuff like, "Don't raise your hand in class! You'll look dumb!"? That's the devil of self-doubt at work. And that negative self-talk can diminish a girl's self-esteem, each and every time.

Following are a few cheer-yourself-on comments to combat the stuff that can bust your self-esteem in a major way. You'll see how to mute your inner devil and pump up the volume when your angel is giving you the good word.

Self-esteem Booster 1 — "I look good, darn good!"

Megan dislikes her hair because she says it's too flat, her nose because it has a bump, and her ears because her friends can wear multiple earrings while she can only wear one in each lobe. Yet here's the thing about Megan —all her friends think she's beautiful.

Even though her friends and her family tell her all the time how pretty she is, Megan only focuses on what she doesn't like about her looks. She doesn't see that her "flat" hair and tastefully adorned ears are beautiful. And the bump on her nose? No one else sees it. Megan has convinced herself she's ugly because she tells herself she's ugly—over and over (and over and over).

Does Megan's story sound familiar? If so, seems like you could also be battling an unnecessary case of the "I'm so ugly" blues. But here's the good news: Even if there are things you don't like about your looks, you can still feel good about yourself. How?

First, cut the mirror inspections. If you spend enough hours scrutinizing your face, you'll start obsessing over the tiniest of imperfections. Instead, listen to the angel on your shoulder and discover something you *like* about the way you look. Perhaps you have pretty eyes, or textured hair that looks great in a sassy short 'do. Or

maybe you have lips that are gloriously lush and full, or your nails are great, or whatever. We promise there is something lovely about you. Focus on what's pretty, and soon even your so-called flaws will become great, unique features.

Self-esteem Booster 2 — "I'm one smart cookie!"

Ever been put on the spot in class? As in, the teacher asks a question and you let the devil of self-doubt convince you that you don't know the answer, so you don't raise your hand? Even though the darling angel tried to get your attention you chose to listen to that negative "what if?" ticker-taping in your head.

So what if you raise your hand and actually give the wrong answer? Would a loud, rude buzzer go off as though you'd just lost it all on a game show? Of course not. The next time your inner voice poses a negative "what if?" query, answer the little devil with a tenacious "as if!"

Self-esteem Booster 3 — "I can do it!"

It's usually no biggie to conjure up your confidence when you're doing stuff you've already done before. But when you have to try something new—go out for softball, style your hair into a brand new 'do, or approach that cutie in class—it's a little more sweat-inducing.

The reason that trying new stuff inspires the little devil to whisper failings in your ear? Fear. Sometimes fear subtly convinces you that you're better off not breaking new ground. "Why take the risk?" it asks. Other times, fear tells you straight up, "There's no way, girl!" No matter how fear presents itself, its message always translates to, "I can't do it."

So, how do you avoid such insecurity? Take a lesson from *The Little Engine That Could*. The unhappy engine couldn't climb the hill because he convinced himself he couldn't. But when he repeated to himself, "I think I can, I think I can," he cleared the hill with no problem.

When you're faced with a challenge, and all you can hear is, "I can't do it!", close your eyes and say, "I know I can do it," 10 times. Then, keep repeating it to yourself, until you've signed your name to the softball tryouts list—or smiled and said, "Hey," to that cute boy.

If you don't go for it, you'll never know if you've missed something amazing. If you take the plunge and end up hating the team, the boy, or the haircut, at least you'll be over it. (Hey, hair grows back, ya know.)

Self-esteem Booster 4 — "Happiness is not about being popular!"

Some girls have everything. Also, pigs have wings and fly around the moon at midnight. Now, can we get serious? Nobody has everything! "The popular crowd at my school is different than on TV because they're really nice, which makes it hard not to like them," says Cary, 12. "They don't dress fancy. They just dress casual in, like, jeans and cool tees. And they all say 'hi' to whoever says 'hi' first without acting like it's such a big deal to know them."

Popular people are usually beautiful and adored, and we all want to feel beautiful and adored. But here's one of the best-kept secrets in history: Popular girls have their own list of insecurities, too. So, if your doubting devil is telling you, "I wish I were more like the popular girls," listen to your angel because she's telling you you're great the way you are.

Believing you're beautiful, well-liked, smart, and worthy of doing cool things all starts with *telling* yourself you're all those things. So isn't it time for a personal pep talk?

When you're growing up, it's sometimes hard to appreciate the life you have. Yes, living by the rules can be a bummer and can make life seem like less than a bowl of cherries, but—and please don't hate us for saying this—strict parents are good parents. Girls with folks who let them run wild typically have problems in school, trouble dealing with authority, and other headaches in life you don't want.

Maybe you're wearing out this tired statement: "I never get to do anything." But what do you expect life to be? A cola commercial? Remind yourself how lucky you are to have parents or grandparents or other guardians who care enough about you to set limits.

UP YOUR CONFIDENCE QUOTIENT!

OK, you know you rock. What's next? Letting the rest of the world know how glorious you are! Very few girls can just glide through life, seeming totally sure of themselves in any situation. It's a skill that's learned. Class is now in session....

How can I be confident when meeting new people?

Say you joined the yearbook staff. You walk into your first meeting, and a group of girls are chatting and laughing together. You recognize a few faces, but you don't really *know* anyone. Do you walk over and jump right in? Or do you quietly take a seat in the corner?

Nervous Nelly says: Never draw attention to yourself. Stand far enough away so you don't bother the other girls, but close enough

so one or two of them can see you. Keep your eyes down so they don't think you're being nosy.

Confident Chica says: Nice try, but staring at your feet and pretending you don't see the group won't fool anyone. Plus, nobody wants to talk to someone who looks uncomfortable or,

worse, *uninterested*. Instead, grab a seat near the girls, and make eye contact with the one who's talking. Smile and show that you're interested, but don't try to steal the spotlight. Wait for someone to introduce you to everyone, or do it yourself when there's a lull in the convo. Smile and say, "Hi, I'm Emma." Then, jump into the discussion, throwing in comments like, "Wow, that's amazing!" and, "Really?" or, "What happens next?"

I totally goofed, and I feel like a big dork. Now what?

A little spit sprayed on someone from the popular group when you laughed at her joke. You barged into a conversation like a buffoon. Now what? Can you join the Witness Protection Program? Will your parents agree it's time to move— tonight?

Nervous Nelly says: See? Being confident is full of potential disasters! Back under that rock.

Confident Chica says: No one is super-smooth all the time! Apologize if necessary: "So sorry for spraying it instead of saying it. Don't you hate when that happens?" But don't go on and on about it. Saying something as simple as,

"Smooth move, (your name here)," takes away any awkwardness and shows you're confident enough to accept yourself for who you are— flaws and all. So keep your head up, and cut yourself some slack. Even the Queen of The Social Scene trips up every now and then.

How can I get my voice to stop squeaking when I'm nervous?

Every time you try talking when your crush is around, your voice squeaks and cracks? Yikes! This is a telltale sign you're freaking out. Is there a way you can stop your voice from sounding like a high-pitched whistle?

Nervous Nelly says:
Eek! If that happens, don't talk at all. Just smile and hope nobody asks you any questions.

Confident Chica says:
Yeah, right, and miss out on making a crush connection? Try this: Each morning in your room, hold a pillow to your mouth, and talk in a nice, full voice. Or sing along with the radio as you get dressed for school. If you were in a weightlifting contest, you'd build up your muscles, right? Think of this as building up your vocal chords to have a squeakless conversation with your crush or smooth answers when you have to speak up in class.

I feel so awkward and ungraceful, even if I'm just walking around.

Do you walk with your arms across your chest, shoulders slouched, eyes down? If so, how can you wonder why people don't smile at you and say "hi"? A confident walk speaks for itself. Even if you're feeling a little shy, nobody will ever guess it.

Nervous Nelly says:
But, if you walk quietly, with your eyes down, nobody will bother you.

Confident Chica says:
Walking around like everything's a drag definitely makes you look insecure. So strut your stuff like you're in control—it makes a

difference. Relaxing your body is the easiest way to calm your nerves. Take a deep breath, and walk tall—head up, shoulders back, eyes forward. Let your arms swing freely at your sides. Practice until it feels natural.

BEING TRUE TO YOU! SELF-ESTEEM RULES

Congrats! Now you know the secrets to feeling good about yourself and projecting that new confidence to the world. But there are tough times and situations that can test any girl, wreaking havoc with your self-esteem and confidence. One of the big things you need to realize is that remaining true to yourself while pleasing everybody is almost impossible. But no girl should ever feel bad about putting her own needs and happiness first.

Yes, you are a wonderful and giving person—we're not telling you not to be. We're simply reminding you that there will be times and situations in which you should look out for *numero uno*—YOU!

Going for the Gold

"I've been running for the past five years, and I love it. It's something that comes naturally to me, but I also practice all the time. I'm thinking of joining the track team this spring, but I don't want to compete against other girls in my grade. I worry that if I outrun them, they'll go around believing that I think I'm so great. I want to compete and do my personal best, but I don't want other girls to hate me for it."

Rule #1: Don't keep yourself down to help others feel up.

Competing sometimes means beating. It's either you or your opponent. You should feel proud, even awesome, when you win, especially given the time and energy you put into becoming a great athlete.

Your competitors might not always be thrilled about your victory. Hey, they could even be bummed out about it. But that's not your problem, as long as you're not gloating and riding the "title" wave. You should always do your absolute best. True athletes show good sportsmanship and respect your efforts. So if you come in first at the finish line, shake hands, wish them well, and race off to celebrate!

Competing for the Same Spot

"I've been thinking about running for school pres in the next student government election. I'm not just doing it to be popular; I have some cool ideas on how to make the school better, and I'd like the leadership experience. But here's the thing. I have to run against this girl I know. Is it mean to run against her?"

Rule #2: Take care of you, and let others take care of themselves.

Let's get this straight—no one should ever try to stop you from striving for something good. It's so cool that you want to be a leader and that you feel confident you have the skills to make a difference in your school.

Unfortunately, sometimes girls hold themselves back from going for their goals the very second they think someone might take offense.

The best you can do is run an honest race and sink all your efforts into winning. You've got our vote—now start hanging those campaign posters!

Standing Up to a Whole Group

"My science teacher divided the class into groups for a project. We were supposed to do a presentation on an endangered species. Well, I was worried about my group from the beginning because they're all pretty lazy and unmotivated. When we sat down for our first meeting, I was the only one who had any ideas. Second time, same thing! I knew I'd end up doing all the work, which is exactly what happened. We still have several weeks left until the presentation is due, and I'm frustrated. I want to tell them how unfair this is, but they'll think I'm a jerk."

Rule #3: Nice doesn't mean keeping quiet while others step all over you.

It can be difficult enough standing up to *one* person who is taking advantage of you, but a *whole group*? Especially if they're kids you have to see in school every day. But let's get real. Staying silent and continuing to take on all the work is totally unfair. If you get a crummy grade, you'll be bummed because you'll know it was too much work for you to have done alone. If you score an A, you'll resent knowing that you and *only you* deserved it.

Sometimes you might avoid telling others you're ticked because you think it's not nice to upset them. Nice? This has nothing to do with nice! This has to do with standing up for yourself when you are being used.

If you tell the kids in your project group that you're feeling dumped on, they might feel upset, guilty, or even angry—which is fine. They are, after all, responsible for their own inconsiderate actions. But here's a suggestion: At the next group session, announce all the different tasks that need to be done to wrap up this endangered species thing. Volunteer for one, and then ask the others to pick what they want to do. If no one follows through, it's time to talk to your teacher about the problem.

Challenging Authority

"I am on this really good traveling gymnastics team and my coach said something really mean to me the other day. She said my leotard looked too tight and it was obvious I was 'slacking off.' She said it in front of all the girls, and I was totally humiliated. Then, everyone started practicing their routines and seemed to forget all about it. But I can't forget. I want to let my coach know how horrible she made me feel. But I'm worried that if I do, she won't help me as much with my routines."

Rule #4: Say what's on your mind when someone has wronged you—even if that someone is an adult.

Let's see. Part of being a gymnastics coach (a big part) should be about raising the team's confidence instead of stomping all over it. It's terrible that your coach made such a lame comment—and in front of everyone! If you don't say something to her ("Hey, your comment the other day really hurt me"), you are actually giving her permission to treat you, and other girls, like that again.

By telling her (in a respectful way) that you're offended, you are letting her know you deserve to be treated with respect, too. If she has an ounce of decency, she'll apologize on the spot and mend her ways. If she refuses to acknowledge your feelings, she's probably not someone you should be putting your faith in anyway. If she shuns you because you stood up for yourself, wave buh-bye and back handspring off to another gym.

QUIZ
Assert Yourself!

Wish you could always say what's really on your mind? You're not alone. Many girls find it hard to be confident—to express their feelings, wishes and needs so others will listen. How assertive are you? Check out this quiz and find out.

1. You and a couple of buds are chowing down at a favorite local diner. You order a well-done burger, and the waitress brings you a slab of raw meat. You:

a. mask the flavor with mounds of condiments. The waitress is busy and doesn't need you bugging her.

b. figure it's time to become a vegetarian.

c. ask the waitress to please bring the well-done burger that you ordered.

2. The computer mistakenly prints out your name on the school's unexcused absence list. You head straight to the principal's office and:

a. calmly report the error to make sure the mistake gets fixed.

b. mumble in denial while studying the cracks in the floor tile.

c. feel so sick about it that you immediately re-route yourself to the nurse's office.

3. You've planned a sleepover with two girls from your tennis team. When your best friend asks if you can baby-sit that night for her kid brother while she goes to a concert, you:

a. cancel your sleepover. What are friends for?

b. tell her you have plans and aren't sure you'd want to baby-sit her brother anyway, but offer to help her find someone else.

c. tell her you'd be glad to sit, but you've been exposed to the Mediterranean Fruit Fly virus.

4. **Your bud shows up smiling with her new 'do—best described as the "poodle" look—and asks what you think. You:**

a. pretend to get sidetracked by a UFO.

b. tell her she looks like a supermodel. Why make her feel bad?

c. say, "It wouldn't work on me, but do you like it?"

5. **Your two best friends are planning to go skating early Saturday, but it seems they've forgotten you're still hobbling around on a sprained ankle. You:**

a. shrug it off. You're the one who thought the "Slippery When Wet" signs didn't apply to you.

b. ask if they'd mind going to a movie and postponing skating until next weekend. Your ankle should be healed by then.

c. sigh, roll your eyes, and sarcastically announce, "Sounds like fun—for those who can skate."

6. **For the third time this month, a pal begs to copy your math homework so she won't flunk. You:**

a. hand it over.

b. hand it over—but only if she promises to take you up on your offer to be her tutor for the next unit.

c. tell her you'd rather not because it makes you feel uncomfortable.

7. **Your science teacher divides the class into groups for projects. There's tons of work to do, the project's due in three days, and everyone says they can't meet because they have all sorts of stuff planned. You:**

a. get used to the idea of an F. If you work hard, you should be able to bring up your average before the end of the year.

b. get to work! You have three days to save the project, your grade, and everybody else's hides.

c. call an emergency group session and ask everyone to help devise a plan.

8. **It's the school election. You seem to be the only one in your group who wants the girl who can add to be class treasurer. At lunch, everyone is raving about the other candidate's wardrobe. You:**

a. snicker under your breath. If no one notices, shake your head and mutter.

b. pretend you're voting for Miss Best-Dressed. You don't want everyone to make fun of you for choosing the other girl, do you?

c. say you agree her duds are killer, but prefer to vote for the girl you think will do the best job.

Take a look at the answers below and give yourself one point for each question you answered correctly. As you tally, note the italicized "rights." If you're having trouble being confident, check out the tips in the following section on how to be more confident and assertive.

1. (c) You don't want to be a pain, get the waitress in trouble, or make a scene. *But you* do *have the right to ask for what you want.* And to get what you pay for. So if your burger is going, "Moo," ask for a new one. *Just be polite about it.* The waitress will probably appreciate your manners and bring it to you faster. However, if your lettuce was not dried to your liking—deal.

2. (a) Many girls feel self-conscious whenever their principal (or any adult) says something that might be wrong. It's easy to think, "What if I say something dumb?" What if you do? The world will not come to a crashing halt. The more you worry, the more nervous you'll get and the less clearly you'll think. *Say to yourself, "I might be a kid, but I have the right to challenge info that's incorrect." You also have the right to ask for information from adults.* So hold your head high, look them in the eye, and say what you need to say.

3. (b) It's hard to say "no" to a friend. But that doesn't mean you have to give up your life for hers. *You have a right to set your own priorities.* If you think she'll be angry, it might be time to rethink the friendship. *Your feelings are as important as anyone else's.* Be direct and honest. If you feel OK about saying no, you won't be as tempted to make up some excuse, and your friend should appreciate your honesty.

4. (c) When a close friend asks for your opinion, assume she wants an honest one but not one that'll hurt her feelings. What if you tell her you love her 'do, and she's so pleased she perms it again? On the other hand, saying she looks like a freak won't score you points either. *Be as kind and as truthful as possible.* You can *always* find something nice to say.

5. (a) or **(b)** If it means a lot to you, ask your friends to consider changing the plans. *You have the right to ask for what you want.* They might go ahead without you anyway—which is their right. *You also have the right to choose not to assert yourself.* If you decide to speak up, use words. Sarcasm and eye-rolling don't cut it.

6. (c) Many girls do things they don't want to because they fear upsetting others. But it's important not to do anything against your values. *You have the right to say "no" without feeling guilty.* If you do things that seem wrong, you'll feel bad and maybe even get in trouble. Express your feelings to your friend without lecturing her.

7. (c) It might seem easier just to do the group's work yourself. *But it's your right to refuse to be taken advantage of.* If you don't like doing more than your fair share, don't complain or whine. Simply tell them.

8. (c) Disagreeing with friends is healthy. Rejecting their choice for treasurer doesn't mean you're rejecting them. Besides, an election is a good opportunity to spark debate. *You have the right to express your own opinions.* But it's not assertive if you express your opinions indirectly or non-verbally. It's also not assertive if you convey your thoughts by putting down others' opinions. *Express your feelings clearly so others will take you seriously.*

Scoring

Give yourself one point for each situation you addressed correctly.

If you received 6 to 8 points: Congrats! You clearly know how to tackle some sticky situations. You have the right attitude and skills to handle confrontations. Keep up the good work.

If you received 3 to 5 points: You're on the right track, but your confidence quotient could use a little work. Practice responses to the conflicts you face most often, and you'll be well on your way to a confident you.

If you received less than 3 points: You need to work hard on changing your attitude and communicating your thoughts. The good news: With practice, you can become just as assertive as anyone else.

Everyone knows someone whose behavior makes you cringe. Nothing is ever good enough for her. Take her into a restaurant and a minute after ordering a salad, she barks, "What is taking so long—did they have to go out back to grow it themselves?"

After observing her obnoxious behavior, if a waiter brings you yellow pencils instead of fries, you'd rather eat them than sound anything like her. But before you risk lead poisoning, listen up: There's a difference between being annoying and being assertive. Obnoxious behavior ignores other people's feelings, while assertive behavior considers how the message affects the listener. Here's how to be more assertive:

❀ **Be specific, direct, and clear.** Others can't read your mind, so it's your job to clue them in. Get to the point quickly. If you're surprised by a test the day you return from a weeklong illness, tell the teacher you were sick and ask for a make-up. Don't make excuses about your fever, how you tried to get the assignments, etc.

❀ **Stop apologizing.** By saying, "I'm sorry to bother you, but..." you're sending a message that you don't think you have the right to take up the other person's time. Trying to get someone's attention? Try, "Excuse me..." or, "Have a moment?"

❀ **Use good body language.** Look straight into the listener's eyes. It detracts from your message when you're staring at the fuzz on the principal's pants. Stand still in a relaxed position, and use a firm voice. No whining, begging, or baby talk. If you hear yourself saying "um" a lot, take a deep breath and focus on what you want to say. And take your time— mumbling is bad, and speed talking is worse.

❀ **State your request.** Let's say a group of kids is sitting behind you at the movies, making all sorts of noise. Turn around and say, "I can't hear the movie. Please, be quiet." Use a serious tone, and don't wait so long to say something that you're ready to explode. If they don't respond, calmly repeat the same message so they know you mean business. If it still doesn't work, you might have to get the usher or consider changing seats, but at least you stood up for your right to hear the movie you paid for.

✿ *Stay focused.* Sometimes, no matter how assertive you are, your listener will refuse to see it your way, leaving you two choices. You can drop the issue and try again later. Or you can be more insistent. Remember to keep your cool and avoid getting sidetracked into other arguments. For example, a boy in your grade asks you to pass a pack of cigarettes to the girl whose locker is next to yours. There are teachers roaming the halls, and if you get caught holding cigarettes, you could find yourself on an unscheduled vacation. You say, "Sorry, but I don't want to." He responds with, "What, are you some kind of goody-goody?" Resist the temptation to prove you're not. Just repeat the message exactly as before: "Sorry, but I don't want to." He will have no choice but to realize you're not going to back down.

✿ *Practice, practice, practice.* You are ready to assert yourself. Begin practicing in easy situations to build your confidence. Before long, you'll be experiencing sweet success. You'll also be more aware of those who are great at being assertive. Learn from their behavior, and try out some of their strategies. Finally, always remember to mean what you say—and say it like you mean it!

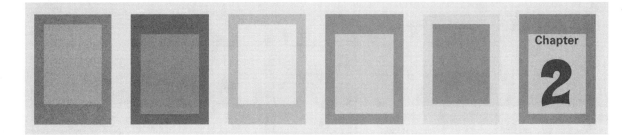

FITTING ROOM

Body Image: Sizing Up the Skin You're In

Body Image: Sizing Up the Skin You're In

While some girls might slip into their swimsuits or new holiday dresses and smile, other girls size themselves up in the mirror and cringe. Maybe it's just for a moment or two. Maybe it's for a lot longer. But the truth is, how you feel in that tankini or that velvet number rests on one important thing—your body image. A lot has been written, said, and debated about girls and body image. What everyone agrees on is this: At some time or another, most girls become convinced their bodies don't measure up. And, of all the different factors that are tied to your self-esteem, body image is a biggie. That's why you need to know how to keep your body image in buff shape.

MIND OVER BODY

The first step in toning up body image is realizing where you're getting your messages and ideas about your body to begin with.

In other words, when you peer into that mirror and size up how you feel about your looks, what are you basing that on? Messages from your folks? Comments from your friends? Ideas from magazines, models, or TV? Sure, you'd like to think the way you feel about that body in the mirror is based on your own opinion. But could it be that someone or something else is helping you decide?

Messages from Parents

You have your parents to thank for a lot of things. One of them is the genetic code that gives your body its blueprint—whether you're short or tall, have long limbs or a short stature, blue eyes or brown ones.

If you think you take after your mom, most scientists would probably agree. You might get height from your dad's side of the family or even his great blue eyes, but when it comes to things like hips, breasts, and overall body shape, you are more likely to take after your mom as opposed to one of your dad's female relatives. Chances are, your mom has been in your skin…almost literally.

What does this have to do with messages about your body? A lot, it seems. While plenty of girls are blessed with moms who can't stop telling them they're fine just the way they are (no matter how much their daughters might disagree), other girls are told by their moms to diet, work out, and quit the junk food. Bad advice? Well, no. Having an active lifestyle and eating a balanced diet are good for anybody. But the difference is the way these suggestions are made. Some girls say their mothers have even called them "fat," "chubby," or "pudgy."

Don't get us wrong—part of a mother's job is to look out for her daughter's health. But messages like those can crush a girl's confidence. Before you go thinking these moms are mean, understand that they usually say such things out of concern for their daughters' well-being. Many moms fought their own battles with the bulge and now worry that their daughters will face a lifetime of dieting, cruel comments, and prejudices. Most moms would do anything to spare their daughters the pain they might have felt as overweight teenagers. Your mom might see the scale-watching and small portions as a way to spare you. Still, the comments can devastate.

So how can girls encourage their moms to help, not hurt? First of all, remember that your mom loves you and only wants the best for you. Telling you to trade in some candy bars for carrots is simply smart eating. But it's up to you to let her know that you can make healthful food choices. If you feel you are at a healthy weight but your mom has concerns, why not make a trip to the doctor and ask for some guidance? Your doctor will take other factors into account that neither you nor your mom might have thought of (like, those extra 10 pounds will come in handy when you grow six more inches). She can also help you with what kind of diet, if any, you should follow.

It'll also help to have a heart-to-heart with your mom. Was she ever "fat"? How did she feel about her body when she was growing up? How does she feel about it now? You might find that a lot of what she says is based on her own negative feelings, and that she doesn't even realize how her words affect your feelings about yourself. Let her know how happy or unhappy you are with your body, and then ask her to help you come up with constructive ways to help you stay positive. And if you both are dealt your grandmother's ample waist or generous build, why not use it as an excuse for some good ol' fashioned mother-daughter bonding? Biking together, looking for skinless chicken breast recipes, and toasting each other with fruit shakes when you forgo the fudge chunk sundaes for dessert are great ways for you *both* to feel better about yourselves.

Messages from Friends

Nothing beats having a best friend with whom you can talk to about anything and everything—and that includes how you feel about your body. Ideal friends value you for who you are, not how you look. After all, a friend is hardly a friend if she's talking you down all the time. But here's the funny thing. Want to know who talks you down to your friends the most? You do!

Most girls have been told that no one likes a bragger, right? So, when you pipe up to your BFF, "I am so fat. I could never sit next to you—you look *sooo* cute," two things are really going on here. One—you want her to feel good. Two—you are asking her to make *you* feel good by saying what you know is going to be the next thing out of her mouth: "Oh, get out! You look awesome. Now me, I look like a whale!" And so it goes until everybody swears they are the fattest thing around.

It's what we call "the old compliment/complaint exchange." You say how great a girl you just met looks in her outfit, so she compliments you on how nice you look in yours. Then you complain about something you hate about yourself, and she confesses she should've bought the long black skirt instead of the mini dress because she just hates! hates! *hates*! her knees. And the next thing you know, the two of you are off to the friendship races. Girls are lucky enough to be able to rely mostly on their communication skills, but part of that communicating results in a sort of false modesty.

If you indeed have pride in your appearance or are even mildly pleased with yourself, why can't you just say, "Thanks," when your friends tell you how great you look?

The fact is that conversations with friends can make a totally positive difference if you feel good about yourself. "I weigh a lot more than my friends," says Alison, 12, "but they remind me that most of my body is muscle because I am more athletic than a lot of people. Although I sometimes say I feel fat, I know I'm really not."

We all know it's who you are that counts, not what you look like or what size you wear. So making fun of anyone for being overweight is just plain mean. "I don't like it when someone is made fun of because of her weight," says Meredith, 12. "You can't control genetics. My two BFFs are tall like I am, but we are all built differently. I am stronger than the two other girls, so I have more weight. One of the girls is really thin, and the other is a little overweight. And that's OK."

The bottom line? When it comes to influencing your fit body image friends can be your best coaches. They can fend off any negative messages because they know the truth—your value is in who you are as a person. If they don't tell you that or act in that way, they aren't *really* your friends. They are insecure and need to put down others to make themselves feel better.

Friends come in all shapes and sizes. Take a good look around any group, and you'll see a variety of heights, weights, and stages of development. Wouldn't it be boring if everyone had the same type of body? And weird!

Media Madness

Every day, you are bombarded with images. They beam at you from TV sets, stare back from magazine pages, and look down from billboards. It seems you can't turn on the tube or open a fashion magazine without seeing a posse of skinny models. When people criticize the media, it's mostly for presenting girls with body types that are unattainable in real life.

"I know I'm not going to look like any of those models," says Trish, 12. "Models are models for a reason, and there is a reason there are so few of them. Real people don't look like that. I just kind of tune them out. I still like to look at fashion magazines, but it's not like I think anyone should look like them—least of all me."

Hear the truth: Models have hair and makeup people who help them look great, and their photos are touched up to make their legs look thinner, their skin clearer, and their eyes brighter.

Still, many girls open up magazines and think, "I'd love to have her body." It kind of stinks that the media reinforce the idea that having a desirable look means being tall, super thin,

and having legs like a giraffe. Call it a culture thing. As a country, we've made great strides in appreciating all aspects of our national diversity. Why, then, do we still think tall and thin is in? In many parts of the world, what passes for a "model" body would strike people as sickly.

Realize that the world is made up of tons of different body types and yours is one of them. Look around you and see that people of all body types can have friends, lead active lives, and generally have a great time. And if you're idolizing and envying media celebrities for their

"perfect" physiques, stop right now. As for media images that push you beyond being entertained to questioning how you look and feel, tune 'em out. Now, *that* is mind over body!

SIX SECRETS TO A KILLER BODY IMAGE

Now that you're more in tune with where you get messages and ideas about your body image, learn to appreciate and work out what you love most about your unique physique. Here are six secrets for boosting body confidence, plus real talk from real girls about how they keep their body images in check.

Secret #1
An air of confidence goes a long way.

True confidence comes from choosing not to worry about things you can't control. While you're probably active and healthy, you also know that genetics play the biggest role in how your body looks. And since life doesn't come with a "reset" button, why not focus your energy on the things you like about yourself instead?

✿ "I have a growth deficiency, so I'm really short and flat-chested for a 13-year-old. But for the most part, I am OK with it. There are odd days when I think it stinks, but then I forget about it and just go have fun with my friends, read a good book, go on the computer, or whatever. It really bums me out when my friends complain about their bodies. We should all realize we're goddesses in our own way!" —Rachel, 13

✿ "You can have an awesome bod, no matter what! All you need is a big dose of confidence, confidence, confidence. I definitely do not have a perfect body. Who does? Last year, I was down on myself because I'm totally flat-chested. Then I realized that I can eat as much as I want and not gain weight. All you have to do is find something you like about yourself and then make the most of it." —Megan, 14

Secret #2
Envy is a waste of time.

You know that saying about how the grass is always greener on the other side of the fence? Same is true for bodies—flat girls want breasts, short girls want to be tall, and so on. So the next time you look in the mirror and are about to slam yourself, remember that there are plenty of girls who see your "flaw" as an asset!

✿ "Sometimes when I shop for pants or skirts, I don't feel so hot about myself. I usually wear one size up from most of my friends. I try not to feel so self-conscious because I know I'm a lot taller than most of my friends. I also remind myself that as long as I'm healthy, it doesn't matter what size I am." —Jen, 12

✿ "Here's a lesson I learned from some girls in my class: I was really jealous of them, but then I found out they were also jealous of *me*. You might not be a supermodel, but remember that everyone has at least one great body feature." —Jackie, 11

Secret #3
The bottom line is people like you for who you are, not for your size.

It seems so obvious, doesn't it? Would you stop loving your sister or BFF if she weighed 10 pounds more? Didn't think so! It's a sad thing that so many girls get bummed about themselves when their bodies go through natural changes. So next time you start to criticize yourself, instead try to think, "Hey, lots of people love me just the way I am." Show yourself the same care and respect that they do.

✿ "I'm not perfect, but when I look in the mirror, I think, 'I'm looking pretty good today.' I don't worry too much about my appearance. My friends are my friends, and they like me because of my personality—not my body! Whether you're big, small, short, tall, or whatever, don't get upset with yourself about your size. It's not worth it. If you have friends who like you for you—that's all you need." —Alina, 12

✿ "Body confidence comes from my friends being supportive. My friends never say mean things about my appearance. If they did, they wouldn't be true friends."
—Laura, 11

Secret #4
Healthy eating and fitness habits go a long way.

Let's get one thing straight: The goal of working out and eating right is not to turn yourself into a stick figure. But study after study proves girls feel better about themselves if they devote time to regular exercise—anything from team sports to dancing around your bedroom for 20 minutes a day—and eat a balanced diet that includes all the food groups.

✿ "My body image changes as fast as my actual body morphs! It all depends on how I feel that day. Some days, I look at myself and say, 'I'm looking so good right now.' Other days, I say, 'Molly, you should really tone up that tummy!' After I've exercised, I automatically feel better. I recommend this to everyone. It makes you feel refreshed, healthy and energetic."
—Molly, 13

✿ "I play soccer a lot, and it helps me stay in shape. And while other people snack on potato chips, I munch on fruit. Want to feel great? Just eat healthy foods and stay active." —Hanna, 12

✿ "Snacking really packs pounds on me, so I came up with a solution. Every time I want a candy bar, I chew sugar-free gum instead. And thank goodness for my dogs because I can get them to go for a long run with me every day."
—Christy, 11

Secret #5
Think like a boy.

OK, studies *do* show that boys are worried about the way they look, too. But, honestly, how many boys do you know who spend half the day complaining about how fat their thighs are? Not many! For the most part, boys don't openly obsess about this stuff. They have better things to do—and so do you!

❧ "I'm pretty much a tomboy. I like to play sports, skateboard and listen to music with positive messages. As a result, I don't pay attention to many females who might influence me to want to change my body. I know it's not the answer for most girls, but that's my secret." —Andrea, 13

Secret #6
Don't compare yourself to others, especially celebrities.

Yes, the truth is out: Celebrities have teams of stylists who make sure they look great at all times! And most of them work out like fiends and insist photos be altered to make them appear much better looking than they really are. (All so they can make more money off your admiration of them!)

Why let them take your self-esteem along with your hard-earned cash? Of course, it's a little harder to deal with the school "superstar." But remember that people come in all shapes and sizes, while *you* only come in one. The sooner you're happy with your own special body combo, the sooner you'll feel like a star.

❧ "When people ask me about my weight, I think, 'Oh, no!' Don't get me wrong—I like my body. But what really bugs me is when people hear how much I weigh and then think I'm fat. Muscle weighs more than fat, and I have a lot of muscle from doing karate! No way am I ever going to be super skinny, but I don't let it get to me. I know it's hard not to listen to other people, but I have learned to be satisfied with myself. It only matters what I think of my body." —Karla, 13

❧ "Girls sometimes think they have to look or act like some unrealistic stereotype to be considered attractive. I don't. That's why I have confidence. I don't compare myself to anyone. Instead of thinking, 'This is terrible; I'm so different,' I just remember people who starve themselves or feel they need to wear revealing outfits to get confidence. Then, I'm so thankful I'm not like that." —Dawn, 12

✿ "I've found the secret to feeling good about myself is disregarding what other people look like. Everyone is different—different weights, different chest sizes, different heights, and so on. In the end, I think changing proportions are really what make some teenagers feel fat. Obviously, if you're 5-foot-6 and feel you need to weigh the same as someone who's 5-foot-2, there's gonna be a problem." —Jolene, 12

BONUS SECRET!
Make friends with your body.

Do any activity that gets you more in touch with all the wonderful things your body can do—gymnastics, dance, yoga, whatever. While many girls think the secret to a great body image is avoiding the mirror altogether, it's not. Krista, 12, couldn't be more right when offering the following advice.

"I think a lot of girls don't realize how good they really look. I see myself in a leotard and tights about 21 hours a week because I dance (ballet, modern, and jazz) six days a week. I spend a lot of time seeing myself in those dreaded full-length ballet mirrors along all the studio walls. Frankly, whenever I see myself, I never think my body looks bad, just normal. That constant reminder keeps me levelheaded. I don't get too wrapped up in the 'I'm fat' thing.

"I also make it a point to wear clothes that look good on me! I'm not talking teeny halter-tops. Yes, those things would fit, but that's not the kind of 'good' I mean. I can wear fitted pants because they aren't trashy-tight on me. I can wear tiny sweaters that bigger busted girls don't look as good in. I have good legs for capris and knee-length skirts, so I wear them—and get compliments! But I avoid dresses with a deep V-neck or a seam under the bust because I have no chest! In short, if it doesn't flatter you, don't wear it!

"My last tip for a good body image is good posture! Think about it— those models walk perfectly down the runway. You don't see any of them slouching! I'm not saying you have to look like a fashion model, but walking with your head up automatically makes you appear more confident."

TAKE MY BODY TYPE, PLEASE

While we wish every girl were perfectly satisfied with herself, it's human nature to want what you don't have. Petite girls long to be tall. Busty girls would kill for a lanky bod. Straight-haired girls wish for curls. You get the idea. But feeling good about yourself has to be based on more than having a certain look.

Still think changing your body type would make life a breeze? Do you ever think, "Yeah, I really wish I had bigger curves," "I wish I had more muscular legs," or, "I wish I were taller." Perhaps you've wished for the exact opposite features—a waif-like figure, thin thighs or a chest that barely needs a training bra. It would seem to be the answer to all your problems. Well, it's time to hear the truth from the mouths of "the perfect."

1. The Wish: "I want to be really skinny!"

The Assumptions:

- ❀ You can eat as much as you want.
- ❀ You'll look like a glamorous model.
- ❀ You can wear anything, even string bikinis.
- ❀ All the drop-dead cute boys will like you.

The Reality: **Caroline's story**

What could possibly stink about being naturally slender? Caroline, 12, is happy to tell you. Rail-thin Caroline gets picked on for being super-skinny. Kids call her everything from "Skin-and-Bones" to "Twiggy." "People think they're so funny," she says. "Like this boy in fourth grade who kept saying, 'Turn sideways and stick out your tongue—you'll look like a zipper.'"

But perhaps most annoying is the constant teasing from relatives, who Caroline feels should be more sensitive: "I never get through a family occasion without somebody asking me if my mother feeds me." During holiday dinners, aunts and uncles give her heaping portions of stuffing or pie, saying it will "put meat on your bones." Sometimes, Caroline just wants to scream, "Leave me alone!"

Now that she's in middle school, Caroline's even more self-conscious about her figure. She wants to look more like her friends, who've developed curves. Boys don't help by treating her as one of the guys: "They act like I'm their little sister and drool over girls who have chests." And the insinuation that Caroline has an eating disorder hurts even more. "People think I'm anorexic," she says. "I'm not, but I feel like I have to prove it."

The best thing about being skinny, Caroline thinks, is fitting easily into tight spots like airplane seats and movie aisles. Eventually, she will get a figure. And she's convinced her shape will be a bonus in the future. Her mom, who also was naturally thin as a teenager, has found it a piece of cake to keep trim as an adult. "That's pretty good, I guess," Caroline says. "Something to look forward to."

2. The Wish: "I want a large chest!"

The Assumptions:

❀ You'll look great in your tankini.

❀ Guys will tie up your Call Waiting.

❀ You'll look older.

❀ You'll be treated like an adult.

The Reality: Nell's story

Nell, who just turned 14, is the first to say she got more than she hoped for. "I used to pray for something to stretch my training bra," she confesses. "But all of a sudden, I grew about two bra sizes. And that's when the real problems started." What could be bad about being voluptuous? Well, for starters, Nell finds it hard to buy clothes that fit well. "Everything's made for small or average-sized girls," she says, "so on me, it pulls across the chest." She and her mom never used to have arguments about her wardrobe, but now shopping's become an ordeal. "Whatever I think looks cool, my mom thinks looks trashy. I hate to admit it, but things that look great on my friends make me look like I'm in an MTV video."

It's not hard to imagine the torture Nell goes through with guys. "They stare down at my chest all the time," she says, "which is so humiliating. Sometimes they make these weird noises or rude comments. Like I'm not supposed to notice!" So Nell has taken to wearing huge work shirts or sweatshirts to hide her chest. Although she knows the outfits aren't flattering, they are concealing. "And gym's a nightmare," she confides. "When we do the mile run, I'm always worrying about my chest bouncing."

When a guy talks to her, Nell wonders, "Is he interested in me or just my chest?" Recently she's discovered another sticky situation—people think she's older than she is. Says Nell, "Some boys come onto me like I'm already in high school. Like I'm really gonna go to a senior party!" Nell feels that she's just not ready to deal with this stuff yet—it's way too uncomfortable. "Why can't I just be normal?" she asks.

But the good news is that her pals are starting to catch up. "One of my friends told me about this place for bathing suits where I can get one size on top and another size on bottom. It's great!" Nell's found other stores with clothes that are stylish and fitting, too. "And I guess it's not so bad," she says, "because sometimes I like the fact that I look kind of curvy."

NOBODY WANTS TO BE FAT

What's it like to have a body shape that's not high on anyone's wish list? Such as when someone's overweight? Julia, 13, knows what it feels like:

"Usually, people think it's not obvious when they talk about me, but it is. My mom got me this red dress for a dance, and I looked like a stop sign! I saw some girls talking, and one pointed at me and said, 'You mean the fat girl?' I wanted to disappear. In gym class, I'm the last one to be picked for teams. I hate that. I know everybody's thinking, 'Oh, no, we don't want Julia!' I used to feel sorry for the team that got me.

"I'm always worried about what other people think of my weight. When my friends and I go to lunch, they all get burgers and fries. I wonder, 'If I order fries, will they think it's no wonder I'm fat?' But if I get the side salad with fat-free vinaigrette, I'll stick out even more.

"I avoid some situations because they're not worth the hassle. One of my friends has pool parties in the summer, but I'd never, ever, be seen in a bathing suit in front of other kids. So I make up excuses not to go.

"It's definitely not fun having a weight problem, but it's getting easier. It changed when my gym teacher made me play volleyball. She wouldn't take any excuses, so I had to. I'm strong, so I spike well. I'm on the JV team now, and it's awesome. The exercise is good for me. The best thing is, it's getting easier not to worry about what everybody thinks."

3. The Wish: "I want to be petite."

The Assumptions:

- ❀ You'll always be cute.
- ❀ People will always take care of you.
- ❀ You'll have awesome clothes and adorable shoes.
- ❀ You'll be a great gymnast, ice skater or dancer.

The Reality: Ari's story

"The worst thing about being 4-foot-10 is being the butt of annoying short jokes," says Ari, 12. Aside from the usual nicknames, Ari has heard more than her share of wisecracks like, "Hey, how's the weather down there?"

Asked about the pros and cons of her height, Ari finds it easier to list the disadvantages. When she was younger, she found it hard to go to amusement parks with friends. "You have to be a certain height to go on some rides," she says. "I was too short and felt stupid." Also, people often treat her as though she is younger than she really is. "At camp last summer," she says, "some girls were talking about a scary movie and said, 'Don't say that around Ari. She's too little, and you might spook her.'"

Ari also finds it hard to keep up in athletics. When playing lacrosse, for example, her friends assure her that the only reason she can't run as fast as they can is because her legs are shorter. And (is this starting to sound familiar?) it's hard to find clothes. As Ari says, "The junior clothes are too long, and I don't like clothes in the kids' department. But the things I like aren't proportioned right for me."

It wasn't easy for Ari to think of the good parts about being small. But she does confess to using her height as an advantage from time to time: "I occasionally save money—they'll charge me the child rate for movie tickets and never even ask!" She can also weave her way through tight spots. "I'm able to push my way to the front at general admission concerts," she says, "but I have to be careful because I can get smushed."

4. The Wish: "I want to be muscular."

The Assumptions:

✿ You'll be a sports star.

✿ You're the picture of good health.

✿ Not an ounce of flab is visible on your entire body.

✿ Nobody will pick fights with you.

The Reality: Morgan's story

"I don't get why people want to be muscular," says Morgan, 12. "It's so annoying." She credits being on the swim team with building up her muscles, but she comes from a long line of muscular people. In other words, it's pretty much genetic. One of the hardest things, she believes, is people assuming she's a jock: "They get mad when I don't score in basketball or when the puck gets by me in hockey." Truth is, Morgan's a great swimmer—but just OK in other sports.

Since she was little, Morgan says, "I never had stick legs." But Morgan still struggles with being "bulkier," as she puts it, than her pals. Morgan has to remind herself that her contours are muscles rather than fat. And there's the issue of weight. Even though she knows muscle weighs more than fat, "I still feel awful whenever some girl talks about how much she weighs. It's always like 20 pounds less than what I weigh. It makes me feel like a giant." The mean comments she gets, of course, are less than kind. "Boys are always saying stuff, and that makes me mad," Morgan complains. "Like asking me if I can bench-press 50 pounds. Sometimes I feel like just showing them up, but then they'll treat me like a boy. I want to be like every other girl."

Morgan is starting to realize that boys are teasing her for one main reason—they're jealous! She's strong, she's in shape, and she's everything they want to be. But that doesn't mean she doesn't have to work to stay in shape. As Morgan says, "During the summer, my friends all went to the lake, and we were talking about doing sit-ups for stomach flab. Someone asked me why I would even worry about stuff like that. But just because I'm muscular doesn't mean I don't have to try to stay in shape." Morgan takes comfort in reading about models and athletes who sport muscular bodies and exercise to stay in top form.

So, maybe you're surprised to learn that these supposedly enviable figures are actually a royal pain for those who have them. If you've been using up your birthday wishes, throwing all your pennies in the pond, or hoping like mad for a certain must-have look, maybe you've been wasting your time. Trust us—it's better to accept the body you've been given and make the most of it. Whether you're tall or short, muscular or wiry, you'll look and feel better if your body is toned by exercise and nourished by nutritious food.

But no matter what, it's truly your attitude that counts most. Girls who give off vibes of being ashamed of themselves (eyes peering downward, slouched-over posture) make others uneasy. A cheery personality and great smile can transcend any body type. You only look your best when you *feel* that way.

5 GREAT BODY MYTHS

1. **THERE IS AN IDEAL BODY SHAPE.** Not true—there is no such thing as an "ideal" body. Nor is there such a thing as a body that's the "wrong" shape. Bodies can be thin, curvy, short, tall, smaller on the bottom, thicker in the middle, whatever.

2. **WITH ENOUGH HARD WORK AND EFFORT, YOU, TOO, COULD LOOK LIKE A SUPERMODEL.** Nope. Bone structure and body shape are *inherited*. If you don't have teeny bones and a small frame, you're not going to look like you have teeny bones and a small frame. If you're concerned about whether you are over- or underweight, ask your doctor's opinion. There are formulas for ideal weight based on height and frame that can guide you.

3. **IF YOU DO CERTAIN EXERCISES, YOUR BREASTS WILL GET BIGGER.** Sorry, but there's nothing you can do to change the size of your breasts. Like body shape, breast size is largely inherited, so thank your mother, her mother or, perhaps, your father's mother for how great your breasts look.

4. **MODELS AND OTHER BEAUTIFUL GIRLS ARE ACTUALLY PRETTY DUMB.** Not always. Some people are super bright, others fabulously beautiful. A few are lucky to be both. But there is no absolute correlation between intelligence and beauty.

5. **COMPARING YOURSELF TO ALL YOUR FRIENDS IS THE BEST WAY TO JUDGE YOUR ATTRACTIVENESS.** Wrong! It's one thing to get ideas or share opinions with your friends—it's entirely another to compete with other girls. There will always be someone who's thinner, has a smaller nose, or comes closer to your "ideal" figure than you do. If you let yourself get caught up in envying others, you'll be wasting energy better devoted to your own interests, talents, and self-improvement.

Body confidence! It's how you feel about and view your own body—and it has nothing to do with your size. This quiz will help you measure your own body confidence…and then we'll tell you how to give it a boost.

1. **The idea of shopping for a new swimsuit makes you want to:**

a. twirl around the room. You love picking out the perfect swimsuits to show off your best features.

b. get it over with. You don't mind the bathing suit pursuit, but the idea of being in front of a mirror under those bright dressing room lights is no day at the beach.

c. book a trip to Alaska for the summer.

2. **If you could wear only one outfit for two weeks straight, it would be:**

a. a baby tee, a cute little skirt and strappy sandals.

b. jeans and a top.

c. extra-large PJs with an elastic waist.

3. **When you change for gym class, you typically:**

a. change in front of your locker— no worries.

b. face your locker and dress fairly quickly.

c. barricade yourself in a bath- room stall and bolt the door.

4. **Viewing yourself in the mirror sans clothes is:**

   a. a sight to behold!

   b. tolerable to acceptable.

   c. cruel and unusual punishment.

5. **You would describe your bod as:**

   a. a work of art.

   b. healthy—hey, it does what it's supposed to do.

   c. the bane of your existence.

6. **When you see a photo of yourself, your first thought is:**

   a. "Now there's a gal who got sprinkled with good fortune before birth."

   b. "Some days are better than others, but not too shabby."

   c. "Photographing me is now officially off-limits."

7. **When walking between two close desks in class, you:**

   a. plow right through without hesitation.

   b. walk through sideways, inconspicuously, of course.

   c. avoid the desk space altogether —even if it means taking a lap around the whole room.

Now review your answers and determine the letter you chose most often. Then, read below to see what that means about you.

Body Proud

Mostly A's: Well, look at you, miss! You're one confident cat—whether you have more curves than a road map or fewer than a cardboard box. You like what you see in the mirror and have no prob showing the world you have nothing to feel self-conscious about. As long as you're careful to appreciate your fine self without body-boasting, you have no worries. Continue doing what you're doing—being exactly who you are!

Body Double

Mostly B's: While you might not be strutting your stuff, you do seem to be walking the body confidence balance beam. You have days when you wouldn't mind covering up in baggy sweats, but also days when you decide your body is tiptops. But most days, you don't even give it much thought. And, really, why obsess over your bod? All in all, you feel healthy and strong because you take care of yourself.

Body Bummed

Mostly C's: Time to up that body confidence, sister! The source of your low BC could be one of these confidence zappers: 1) You're genuinely overweight and need to take action to feel better about yourself, or 2) You are perfectly healthy but can't see yourself for what you are. If you suspect you are overweight, stop blaming yourself this instant and ask your mom to make an appointment with your physician, who can put you on a sensible, healthful diet-and-exercise regimen. If you suspect that your problem might be a distorted self-image, try the following tips. Not loving yourself (inside or out) is a huge waste of energy and no way to live your life!

Tips on Boosting Your BC

If you ever feel like your self-image is slipping, check out the following tips for an extra confidence boost.

✿ **Raid your closet.** Go right now, and get rid of all the clothes in your closet that make you feel bad about yourself because they don't fit properly. You know, the sweater that's so tight you can barely breathe or the jeans that are so baggy you could hide puppies in them. If the clothes make you feel bad, get rid of them—give them to your cousin or bag them up for Goodwill. What you might consider your worst clothes might make someone else feel great.

✿ **Stop hiding.** The irony is that the more you try to hide yourself, the more you stick out. Besides, truthfully, everyone else is so worried about their own flaws and hang-ups that it's quite doubtful they're noticing any of yours. If you act confident, people will believe you are confident. And there's no one more attractive than a girl who genuinely feels good about herself!

✿ **Face the mirror.** Yep, close your bedroom door, pull the shades down, shed all your clothes, and stand right in front of your mirror with the lights on and everything. At first, you'll probably take note of all the things you don't like. But stop and force yourself to figure out what you *do* like. It might be your curvy hips, the beauty mark on your shoulder, or the freckles on your belly. Don't get dressed until you come up with at least three or more things you like about your bod.

✿ **Stop talking about it.** One reason girls flip out about their bodies is that they spend too much time chatting with other girls about how they hate their hips, who gained weight, and how many calories are in granola bars. You can say to your friends, "You know what? I feel like we've worn out the subject of weight-watching. Let's talk about something else." Do more active things together, like hiking or biking. If your friends can't stop focusing on body stuff, fly solo or find a new friend, and discover something else to do that doesn't involve worrying about fat content.

A+ for Effort:
School Success

Chapter 3

A+ for Effort: School Success

You probably spend more time at school than just about anywhere else besides home (and it doesn't help that sometimes even one class can feel like eternity!). But seriously, how well you do (or—*gulp*—don't do) in school has a huge impact on how you feel about yourself as a whole. And not only is school a learning institution, it serves as a major backdrop for your social scene. That's why this chapter is a sort of crash course on how to cope with all that school-related stuff that could trip you up. At the very least, you'll get an A+ for effort. Not too shabby!

THE SECRETS TO SCHOOL SUCCESS—MINUS STRESS

While you might work smoothly through your subjects, school isn't always Easy Street for everyone. At times, you're bound to feel overwhelmed by the workload, freaked out about the future, and generally less than thrilled with school.

Although attendance isn't optional, you do get to make some important decisions. You can choose whether you'll allow yourself to get into a total tizzy, worry yourself to pieces, and dread each and every school day. Or, you can opt to have a good attitude about school, figure out how to get through each day as enjoyably as possible, and reap all the benefits you can. The latter sounds better, doesn't it? If that seems impossible to you right now, don't despair. Lots of suggestions are coming your way.

Learning to Manage Your Time

Oh, to be in kindergarten again— story time, show-and-tell, spelling bees, papier-maché, and recess. But when you reach upper grades, you're switching classes, learning more intense subjects, and getting more homework and long-term projects— often from several teachers at once. School is truly more challenging and—not counting some classmates' antics—less entertaining than when you were younger. The biggest challenge—surprise!—is the time crunch. Jaclyn, 10, says, "I had to quit a bunch of extracurricular activities because now I do home-work from after school until bed."

Assignments and tests are more complicated, so you need more time to prepare. Maybe you can relate to Chelsea, 11: "I have to stay up until 11 p.m. just to get my homework done and study for the 100 tests I have the next day!"

To tackle the tick-tock time problem, rethink your priorities. Pick a few after-school activities you truly love, and cut the unnecessary stuff. Achieve a good balance by exercising your mind, body, and social self. Even if you're wild about a dozen different clubs, hobbies, and sports, reality says you must pick and choose. And also carve out some down time for yourself so you can rest, think, dream, and create.

Of course, you'll want to save precious minutes to check e-mail, gab with buds, and watch the tube, but keep an eye on the clock. Telephone, computer, and TV eat up time and energy until you have little left for homework. It's hard to concentrate on the capitals of the Middle East if you're listening to your BFF rant about her maddening crush and answering 423 instant messages!

Realistic Academic Goals

Pressure to stay above C-level grade-wise is a huge burden. Where does this pressure come from? Well, if you think your parents are the only ones to blame—wrong! Many girls are their own worst enemies. Maybe you're like Deanna, 12, who says, "I've always been an average student, but I'm trying to get straight A's." It's great to set goals, but the trick is to make them realistic, specific, and doable. You can't go from being a B- to an A-student overnight, or become totally fluent in Spanish in one semester.

Also, if you're in a high-level class, accept that you might not get the A you could easily achieve in an average class. Make short-term, attainable goals. Instead of planning for college at 12, read as much as you can, learn great study skills, and be proud of your accomplishments along the way.

Pressure from the Parents

Your folks want you to be as successful as possible. Nothing wrong with that. Sometimes, however, that translates into expectations of certain grades—such as nearly all A's. If you believe your parents' academic goals for you are more like wishful thinking, openly discuss your feelings with them. What you and your parents have to decide is this: Are you capable of doing better academically and, if so, what will it take?

A favorite teacher or guidance counselor might be able to offer opinions and support. Maybe she'll say your progress is in line with your abilities. But, if a teacher points out any weaknesses, pay close attention. Following her suggestions can lead to big improvements.

What are your teachers' comments? Do you do homework consistently? Do you participate in class discussions? Is your attitude respectful? Are your study habits strong? If these check out, it will be reassuring to both you and your parents that you're doing your absolute best.

Work with a tutor if a subject gives you major trouble. Or meet with a study skills specialist to help you get organized and on track. Your teacher or guidance counselor will be able to help you find them. Make the most of whatever help is available to you.

And maybe your parents can be persuaded to look at the bigger picture. Ask Mom or Dad what goals they have for you, besides being a good student. Do they want you to be athletic, learn responsibility by doing household chores, or participate in musical groups? If so, you can't focus solely on school. Your success is determined by more than just grades. Effort can and should count for a whole lot.

Pressure From Your Friends

Even friends can put incredible pressure on you. Maureen, 10, says, "My BFF teases me when I get a bad grade. I hate that." Another common problem occurs when teachers hand back tests and papers. A frenzy of classmates asking, "What did you get?" can be embarrassing, especially if your grade stinks. When kids brag, tune them out. Or try, "Let's just keep our grades to ourselves."

Lots of girls say that to be your best, it's good to surround yourself with scholarly types. But beware of comparing yourself to the school's reigning geniuses. Melody, 10, says, "When my friend gets a 93, she'll be happy for hours. How does that make me feel when I've gotten an 87?"

It's a simple fact of life that there will always be people who learn more easily than you do. Better to accept that than to torture yourself. Every student develops at a different rate. Some learn to read early, others late. Some don't blossom until college or later. All you can do is your own personal best.

Getting Beyond Grades

To excel, take an honest look at who you really are. No matter how hard you try, you might never be a nuclear physicist, prima ballerina, or Nobel Prize winner. Really, how many people are? It's a shame to beat yourself up for what's definitely not your fault.

Maybe it seems like it'd be fantastic to be a genius, hot-shot athlete, or star artist, but it's not always all that satisfying. It's far more important to be content with who you are as a person. The grades that appear on your report card every few months matter, but they don't have the final say on who you are.

Even if you're a bona fide genius, it's unlikely you're brilliant in everything. The world would be pretty boring if *everyone* were an academic superstar. While Einstein did a lot, he never made cool music, started a fashion trend, or created an amazing sculpture.

Are you good in sports? A terrific cartoonist? Your school's star actress? Whatever your interests, you owe it to yourself to give it your best effort. School is only one part of your life. That said, it is also *not* OK to blow off a D in math! Even if you'd rather be diving off the high board than dividing mixed fractions, you have an obligation to do your best. Now, get to work, girl!

MORE STRATEGIES FOR SUCCESS

If the work piles up like Mt. Everest even after you figure out a sensible schedule, it's time to get better organized.

- **A PLACE FOR EVERYTHING.** Put assignments, books and other materials in their proper places, even if it's a pain. In the long run, you'll spend less time frantically trying to locate assignments.

- **TIME MANAGEMENT.** Elisa, 11, suggests, "Don't lie to your parents and say you don't have homework, and don't procrastinate—or half of it ends up unfinished." Brittany, 10, wisely advises going to the library a few weeks before a paper is due to compile books, references, and notes. When you feel more in control of your work, you might actually begin to enjoy it!

- **WHAT'S YOUR STUDY STYLE?** While a few people find it invigorating to skip around from subject to subject, it's best to adopt one of two strategies. Some girls say it works better to do the hardest work first, when they have more energy and can pay better attention. Others like to get easier work out of the way and then hunker down to some serious studying. Figure out which way works best for you.

- **STUDY BUDDIES.** Arrange for a few friends to get together for a study session before a big test. Each of you can summarize a chapter and teach it to the others. Teaching someone else can help you better learn the material.

- **BREAK DOWN YOUR GOALS.** Your goals should be meaningful to you. Instead of focusing on an ultimate letter grade, plan to work on your grammar in the next English essay, decide to avoid careless mistakes on the upcoming math test, and promise to finish your lab report by Sunday afternoon. When you set specific and sensible goals for yourself, you'll probably see improvement in your performance and be more satisfied with your work.

- **REWARD YOURSELF.** When all is said and done, reward yourself for good effort! Give yourself a little break or treat. And enjoy the great feeling you get from checking off items on your to-do list.

TEACHERS 101

Every teacher has his or her own personality, teaching style, rules, level of patience, oddities, and bad days—all of which, like it or not, you have to adjust to at the sound of each bell. Some teachers you'll like and admire, and others you won't.

No doubt, you have preferences: A soft-spoken, kindly teacher or a dynamic, entertaining one. A serious, no-nonsense type or a stand-up comic. There is also bound to be something somewhat annoying about every single one of your teachers. Maybe it's the way the art instructor taps his pencil on his hand, or the way Mrs. So-and-so smirks after distributing a quiz.

And if that's not stressful enough, each teacher has his or her own teaching style. One of your teachers might call on every-body and expect lively discussions, but your shyness makes it hard for you to shine when put on the spot. Or perhaps another likes to lecture without interruption, but unless you can ask questions, you get confused and distracted. Maybe you prefer to work by yourself, but your teacher sticks you in groups and expects you to accept lower grades along with your less conscientious classmates.

But despite all this, it's important to remember the most basic fact: It's up to you to make your relationships with your teachers work. You have everything to gain or lose—depending on how you play your cards.

Learn to Adjust

Some of your teachers aren't quite what you expected or, more to the point, what you're used to. Sometimes, you have to switch gears to adjust to each teacher's specific rules and ways of doing things. Helena, 11, says, "My teacher last year was big on open book tests, but my teacher this year freaks if I even have a book on my desk during a test."

Similarly, work that earned stellar grades from one teacher might receive mediocre marks from another. As Heather, 12, puts it, "Sometimes, you have to get used to a whole new system." Whether it's about talking in class, chewing gum, getting a bathroom pass, or bringing a sharpened pencil to class, each teacher has his or her own set of rules. Even if you think they're ridiculous, you have to live with them.

How Bad Is It?

Aside from dealing with rules, at times you and a teacher might mix like oil and water. The critical thing is to ask yourself, "Is the problem important enough to make an issue out of it?" You don't want to address every little annoyance that irks you. If your teacher gives you a grade of 97% and you think you deserved 98%, try to let it go.

But what about when the teacher has affected you in a big way, such as when your feelings are hurt or you feel mistreated? These situations often call for action. Your feelings are saying, "Hey, you'd better do something about this injustice." Katya, 11, was humiliated by her teacher: "I failed the first math test

of the year. I was having trouble with algebra, and my teacher held my paper up in front of the whole class. She said, 'See what happens when you don't study.' I wanted to crawl under my desk."

It's especially important to speak out if your distress dampens your enthusiasm for class or interferes with your ability to learn. For Katya, the decision to speak up to her teacher wasn't easy. After much thinking, Katya felt she'd be increasingly self-conscious in math class. She knew she had to speak up or she'd be resentful. Getting her parents' support helped Katya feel less scared about having a discussion with her teacher, but it still wasn't easy.

Getting Geared Up

Once you decide to face the problem, avoid unnecessary skirmishes. Wait until you're less peeved so you can think straight, and then talk about it with someone neutral.

What do you want to accomplish? Do you want your teacher to stop hurting your feelings or embarrassing you? Do you want him to change a policy that you believe is unfair? Are you asking her to reconsider a grade? Whatever it is, don't hint around and expect your teacher to guess. Say it outright. It doesn't guarantee you'll get what you want, but your teacher should respect you for being direct.

Pick a good time to speak to your teacher, and use a pleasant, firm, and non-argumentative voice. Don't insult or accuse her. And no whining! State how you feel and why, and tell your teacher how you think the issue could be resolved. For example, if you're upset that your teacher yelled at you for taking too long to figure out a division problem on the blackboard, you might say, "I am working very hard in this class, but I get nervous when everyone is watching. When you yell at me in front of everyone, it makes me even more uptight."

Be prepared to elaborate, if asked, and be sure to give your teacher a chance to respond. Don't just say, "You hurt my feelings." Tell him how: "I get upset when you call me 'Shorty.' It makes me self-conscious. I prefer being called by my real name." Rehearse what to say with a parent or older sibling. Ask the other person to pretend she's the teacher and you be yourself. Practice different ways of saying your peace until you feel comfortable. After speaking your mind, if you still feel the teacher doesn't take your concerns seriously, consider asking one of your parents to talk to your teacher, or approach another adult, such as a guidance counselor or principal for help.

Beware of Pitfalls

It's important to say how you feel directly to your teacher so your feelings don't fester inside and cause further trouble. Have you ever asked a friend why she's failing a subject, and she responded, "Oh, because I hate my teacher"? How do bad feelings about a teacher turn into bad grades? They shouldn't—unless you resort to any of the following tactics for handling conflicts with teachers, all of which end up hurting only you:

✿ **"I'm just going to ignore the teacher!"** If you're afraid to stand up for yourself, you might avoid your teacher completely. The thinking goes, "If I don't bother the teacher, she won't bother me." But you lose, unfortunately—because you miss out on the help you'll need for your upcoming geography test.

✿ **"I'll be darned if I do what this teacher says!"** If you dig in your heels and refuse to turn in assignments or study for tests, you're indirectly saying, "I'm angry with you, and I want you to notice." But your teacher can't read your mind and might only see you as unmotivated or lazy. You'll likely get more upset about bad grades, and "hate" your teacher even more. This is a no-win cycle.

✿ **"It's my teacher's fault!"** You might believe a teacher is too hard, disorganized, boring, or unclear. All this might be true, but in the end, you're responsible for your work. Rather than hold on to your frustration, figure out what you can do to make things better.

Bringing in the Big Guns

Sometimes, though, it's not a good idea to handle a problem with a teacher by yourself. Some more serious situations are best dealt with by parents. When Ruth, 12, was expected to take a pop quiz after missing school for a family funeral, she was understandably upset. "My mother said it really wasn't a problem between my teacher and me—it was a matter of school policy, so she called the principal."

Other issues require you to tell a parent or other trusted adult—immediately. If you feel uncomfortable around a particular teacher, male or female, pay attention to your feelings and tell somebody. On rare occasions, a teacher might make a remark about your nationality, gender, background, or disability. Tell an adult who can decide what action should be taken.

Armed with these strategies, you can sort out any disagreements that arise. You can decide what is and isn't important, and how to go about expressing your feelings and requests in ways that will encourage teachers to listen. By dealing with conflicts directly and promptly, you'll use your energy for what really matters in school—enjoying learning.

Score Big-Time With Your Teachers

Like it or not, teachers know what's up. They know who gives the work extra attention, who watches the second hand circle the clock, and who calls them "Godzilla" behind their backs. Not only do they know, but they care. And because they're human, that caring can come off as a reflection...on your report card. Even if you're a genius, your teacher's unlikely to dole out an A if she knows you only as "The Eye-rolling Slouch." It's not too late to straighten up and act glued to her every word. No, this is not a pathetic move toward becoming teacher's pet. Read on.

- **Be there, or be square.** Being a no-show or consistently tardy is no way to score points. Out-of-sight, out-of-mind doesn't apply here—chronic absenteeism only causes you to stand out as the kid with the poor attendance record. And rolling into class after the bell rings is disruptive. Unless you have a legit excuse (the bus broke down), being on time to class every day is a must. If you're ill, make sure your mom writes a note—and it's up to you to collect makeup work as soon as you're back to class.

- **Front and center.** Sitting in the front row can max your facts intake because it's easier to focus when you're close to the action. And all teachers know the "I didn't do my homework so I'm hiding in the last row" trick. At the very least, sitting up close will make you seem more interested even if you aren't—and that's what teachers like to see. It's just basic manners to listen when a teacher talks, even if he/she is rambling endlessly about the Eastern Gray Tree Frog!

- **Speak up.** Go ahead—raise your hand. Asking questions and getting involved not only keeps you from being bored, but it impresses teachers. Lots of them grade for class participation, so don't waste a sec thinking you'll look stupid by asking a question. Chances are, a couple of kids will think, "Phew, so glad she asked about that because it made no sense to me."

- **Charm school.** Teachers favor well-mannered students. Little words like, "please," "thank you," and "I'm sorry," pack valuable punch. More school-specific manners include: not interrupting, asking permission for bathroom breaks, and resisting the urge to nod off.

- **Ya gotta sweat.** Sorry, there are no shortcuts. You've gotta do your homework, complete class assignments, and study for tests. It's tough to get teachers on your side if you're slacking. If you throw a paper together the night before the due date, you're not fooling anyone but yourself. Teachers are trained to tell the diff between shabby, half-baked work and real A+ effort. Stumped? Ask for help. Teachers like that, too.

- **It's all about trust.** You might not know it, but teachers are *not* in it for the money. You're misinformed if you think teachers earn megabucks! Most actually just enjoy spreading knowledge. Trust your teacher to help you, guide you, challenge you...and sometimes maybe even cut you a break.

THIS IS ONLY A TEST

Y ou've studied for days and days, absorbing the facts and figures you'll need for the test. You've read and re-read your notes, and asked your parents and sibs to quiz you from a stack of flash cards. You know the info inside and out, and feel ready to go. So how come the second the test hits your desk, you feel doomed? Sweaty palms, shallow breathing, perhaps the words even seem to fade in and out. It's called Exam Anxiety, and you're far from alone if you suffer from it. What you need are some tools to keep you cool and collected when test time comes around.

Before the test

✿ *Confide in someone you trust about your fears.* It's normal to feel somewhat stressed before a test, and it's not going to help matters if you've bottled up all your worries beforehand. Talking to someone— a teacher, parent, tutor, or friend— is a good way to relieve yourself of some of the burden.

✿ *Be sure you're well rested.* The last thing you want to deal with before taking an exam is lack of sleep. Get to bed on time so you'll be bright and shiny in the morning.

✿ *Exercise.* It's a great way to get rid of nervous energy before the exam—and it's time far better spent than cramming at the last minute.

✿ *When you study, practice timing yourself.* For a lot of students, it's not recalling the info that's so tough, but the pressure of knowing they're being timed. Ask a study

partner to ask you a certain amount of test questions while she times you. That way you can get more comfortable with the whole beat-the-clock concept.

✿ *Chat about the test subject.* It's hard to memorize info you find as exciting as a four-hour French drama without subtitles. See if there's a way to liven things up a bit by talking about the subject with a friend in your class.

❀ *Envision the best.* Too many times, students picture themselves failing or getting a bad grade rather than telling themselves they're going to do well. It's key that you go into a test with a positive state of mind. Picture yourself seeing a big fat A when your test paper is passed back to you.

During the test

❀ *Keep both feet on the floor during the test.* When students get nervous, they tend to swivel, tap their feet, circle their ankles round and round, or giggle. All that movement could distract you from thinking clearly. Keep your feet flat on the ground.

❀ *If you find you're starting to freak, take a moment and look up.* This is not only a way to rest your eyes, but it's a good reminder that there is life outside of this test. Just stop and take a few deep breaths. Assure yourself that this test is only one grade in a lifetime of challenges and adventures.

❀ *Give yourself a gold star.* Rather than kicking yourself if you don't know an answer, reward yourself when you *do.* When you're sure you've answered a question correctly, quickly say inside your head, "Way to go!" before moving on to the next question.

After the test

❀ *No matter how you think you did, give yourself a huge congrats.* You deserve it for getting through a difficult challenge.

❀ *Forgive yourself for answers you know you messed up.* It's healthy to consider whether there are ways you could have done better, but it's pointless to beat yourself up for giving wrong answers. It won't improve your grade, and it's only going to make you feel terrible.

❀ *Know there is help available if you need it.* If you're having trouble with either the material being covered, or even with studying for tests in general, start by talking with your teacher. She will likely be able to help you after class or at least suggest a tutor. Your teacher will appreciate that you're concerned enough about your schoolwork to even ask for help.

❀ *Remember that a test doesn't reflect whether you're smart or a good person.* This is only one exam. When you look at the whole of your life—all of the highs and lows that make you who you are— one bad grade is not such a big deal. However, knowing you can face a tough situation without freaking out will take you a mighty long way.

Sure, getting a D- on a test or forgetting your note cards the day of the big oral report can be a major problem. But some situations even get a whole lot trickier if not handled correctly. Help is here to get you unstuck from stuff that could seem like a bad dream. You might wanna break out your highlighter....

Situation #1—Bad BFF Breakup

You ditched your best bud because of "irreconcilable differences." Now, every time you pass her in the hall, she sends evil glares your way.

Solution: You can't avoid your ex-friend forever. Since you're in the same building during the same hours, there's a pretty good chance that you'll run into each other on more than a few occasions. The energy you'll both spend trying to elude each other day after day can definitely be better spent elsewhere—like on patching things up! Spending the year with one more friend and one less enemy is a good thing. It's never too late to sort things out. Try saying,

"Look, this is obviously awkward for both of us. Why don't we talk things over?" and take it from there.

If that doesn't work: If being best buds again is out of the question, aim for being civil. At least acknowledge her with a nod, and keep walking. If you ended things because she did something appallingly unforgivable, just ignore her icy gaze. As long as you've explained to your ex-bud the reason you ended the friendship, why get sucked into theatrics?

Situation #2—Academic Panic

You've always coasted through a particular subject, raking in good grades with little effort. Now, you're totally lost in what was once your favorite class.

Solution: Cut yourself some slack. Having trouble processing all the info you're bombarded with doesn't mean your brain cells are shriveling. You're not dumb! What *is* dumb is not

asking for help. You have a couple options: 1) Ask a fellow ace student to coach you, or 2) tell your teacher how lost you feel. After all, she is paid to help you learn.

If that doesn't work: Tell your parents you need a tutor. Sure, it might cut into social time, but understanding what's going on in class is so worth it. No more staring at your ankles when the teacher is about to call on someone. Tripping over the appropriate endings for your Spanish verbs really isn't that big a deal—you're just hitting a rough spot. So don't get all frustrated. Do what you have to do to get through, and hang in there.

Situation #3—Sibling Invasion

Your little sis now attends the same school as you, and your parents expect you to be her chaperone. There goes the independent coolness you've achieved. What if she clings to you, or (gasp!) tries to befriend *your* friends?

Solution: Think a sec about how your sib probably feels in a new school. Remember when it was your turn, and you were plagued with thoughts like, "What if I can't find my way around the school?", "What if I can't find any friends?", "What if I can't open my locker?" How great would it have been if you'd had an older sib to show your rookie self the ropes? You don't have to hold hands, but how much effort would it take to ask your little sib how it's going, or if she needs anything? It'll help her gain confidence—a quality she'll need in order to make her own friends.

If that doesn't work: If your sib is driving you batty with neediness, introduce her to some of your friends' younger sibs. The buddy system hookup flopped? Talk kindly to your sib about how lame it is for her to totally depend on you. Explain that if she's going to thrive in her new environment, she has to set up her own world and stand on her own tootsies.

Situation #4—Superglue Buds

A girl you're friends with in band expects you to be best buddies during the rest of the school day. You just consider her your "band friend."

Solution: So, you've befriended someone you wouldn't hang out with in "real life." Can you pretend like you don't know her when you see her in the hallway? No! That is extremely mean and unfair. She'll feel hurt and betrayed—and rightfully so. While you don't have to hang with her 24/7, be friendly, introduce her to your crew, and include her when you can. Who knows? She might fit right in.

If that doesn't work: If you can't find it in you to invite her to hang out with your group (or the girls say, "No way!"), reserve some one-on-one time with her. She demands too much of your existence? Tell her nicely that balancing your social and academic scenes is tricky, but that you'll work to fit in hang time with her. And mean it!

Situation #5—Agony of Defeat

You practiced and practiced to make the squad, only to be rejected. You're totally devastated.

Solution: Not making the team stinks. But rather than wallowing in feelings of rejection, remember that there are tons of other awesome activities out there, or join an after-school rec league instead. If you didn't land that part in the school play, drama club still needs a stage crew. There's also probably a whole roster of clubs and teams you haven't even considered.

If that doesn't work: If you can't shake that bummed-out feeling and are absolutely dying to be part of a particular group, ask the coach what you need to improve on to make the cut next time around. And see if any help is needed. Could you be an assistant manager? A scorekeeper? A stand-in for play rehearsal? Besides getting involved in some way, you'll make a significant impression by showing determination and an ability to take constructive criticism. That's what we call keeping it together!

OUCH! THAT HURTS

Being bullied is more than a tricky situation—it's serious stuff. But when you think of a bully, do you envision a bruiser with a buzz-cut named Butch threatening to give some poor kid the playground smackdown?

Well, there *are* plenty of brutes like Butch around, but there's also another breed of bully—one who doesn't flex muscles to intimidate, but instead declares psychological warfare on any kid who happens to be vulnerable. This kind of bully attacks by tossing insults, starting rumors and forming cliques. What's worse, this kind of bullying is so subtle that it sometimes goes completely unnoticed by other people. Thus a bully can even hide behind the guise of Little Girl Good. And anybody could be her next target. Even you.

Power Play

Some kids are so intimidated by a bully that they go along with her bullying to avoid being the next target. Other kids can be fooled into thinking a bully is the best and the brightest. That's because this brand of bully spends so much time trying to convince herself she's so great that many kids believe it.

Most bullies don't have a single iota of self-esteem. Something (who knows what?) is probably causing the bully some inner pain, so she feels better about herself as long as she is putting other people down. Making fun of a chosen few probably helps the bully feel superior and in control. But until she pinpoints the source of her pain, she will likely continue to hurt inside.

Pickin' Prey

How does a predator pick her prey? Often, it's what we'll call The Ruby Bridges Syndrome. Maybe you know the true story of Ruby Bridges—the first African-American girl to attend an all-white elementary school when federal courts integrated the nation's schools in 1960.

Every day at school, Ruby was seriously taunted and even threatened by both kids and adults—just because her skin was darker than theirs. A kid who stands out as different is an easy target for a bully. Sometimes a bully doesn't even need a reason—she just makes one up. "Brittany's hair looks like the color of dirt," she says, probably because she's really jealous of Brittany's long, honey-brown locks. Too bad the bully can't feel good about herself and realize it's cool not to be a clone.

The Pain

You have to wonder if a bully has any idea of the pain she causes for the handful of kids she picks on. She's usually too self-centered to see that a girl from her gym class didn't try out for softball for fear of being laughed off the field. Or that the boy who plays tuba for the band skips lunch to escape humiliation.

To avoid facing her own inner stuff, a bully creates a false sense of self. She'd be doing herself (and everybody else) a favor by knocking that attitude down a few notches, dropping her pushy persona, and being her true self—not some poser who struts around like she's the queen of the school scene.

The Pretenders

Some girls are bullies by association. They travel in a rat pack with a "head bully" as their commander. These girls don't care what anyone else thinks, and everyone is a potential target for their teasing. They might shove the girl wearing

"I DIDN'T LET THE BULLIES KEEP ME DOWN" BY RACHEL, 12

I was the target of several cruel classmates after I had a seizure a few years ago in class. I'm no longer epileptic, but the concept of being different stuck with me. I've been insulted on the kickball field, in the bathroom, and anywhere an adult couldn't overhear. It was hard sometimes to hold back the tears. This girl Nicole started it. Then this girl Sarah made fun of me, and she was the most popular girl in my grade. They got all the boys to get in on it, too. They made fun of the way I dressed, even if I just had on jeans and a tee. I got my hair cut, and I loved it, but they even made fun of me for that.

I felt left out because everyone called me a dork. My BFF stuck up for me and that made me feel better, but it got out of control. Like this boy Jerry asked to borrow a pencil, and when I handed it to him, he said, 'Ew, I can't touch it. I might get a disease.'

Nicole brought presents to school, like cool erasers, and she'd say, 'Oops. I forgot to buy you one.' I'd just lie in bed at night and cry.

Then I decided being miserable was not going to help my self-esteem. I have goals and I knew putting myself down wasn't going to help me achieve them. So I talked to my mom about it, and she got me some counseling to help me deal with it. Now I've learned to completely tune them out, and I'm happy. I just took up the drums, and I'm really getting into them. If you are being bullied, speak up to your teacher, parent, or principal because they'll help. They helped me.

glasses and headgear. They whisper and stare at students, or outwardly heckle them.

But some of these "followers" are mean only under the watchful eye of the head bully, who has a strong influence over her sidekicks. Girls like this should buck the bully system and be themselves. A lot of hurt feelings would be spared, and perhaps the head bully would even knock off her constant badgering and belittling.

Problem Solving

What we hope you've picked up on by this point is that it's never the victim's fault when someone is being bullied. *It's not about the victim; it's about the bully.* Bullies almost always have problems they're too cowardly to face—jealousy, insecurity, or anger. Now that you understand the "why" behind bullying, realize that these are reasons—*not* excuses. There is no excuse for kids to tease, mistreat, or abuse others. If you see someone being harassed, muster up the courage to say, "Hey! Leave that kid alone!" If you're too afraid this will put you in the hot seat, talk privately to an adult about the problem.

Even though you know this is not your fault, unfortunately, it doesn't always make it easier to

deal with on an emotional level. But we have some practical advice for combating all the bullies in your world:

1. Don't give 'em the satisfaction of a reaction. You don't want them to know it bothers you. They make fun of your shoes? Thank them for the compliment. You trip in the hall? Beat 'em to the punchline and joke about it. If they don't get a negative reaction, it foils their fun.

2. Make believe. There's one thing we want you to fake—just for a while. An air of sheer confidence. Pretend you're in control. Walk with your head high, your shoulders back, and act as if you're not at all intimidated. Eventually, the bullies might believe it and lose interest. And you'll get so used to being this way that it'll become second nature.

3. Talk yourself up. Don't let bullies brainwash you into believing you're a loser. You're not! You're a great girl who would never stoop to their level, right? Keep telling yourself there is nothing wrong with you, and that they are the ones with the problem— because they are.

4. Keep your distance. Do your best to avoid bullies altogether. Don't go to the pizza place where they hang in packs. Try the new sushi place instead.

5. Remember, safety is in numbers. Thugs are less likely to single you out if you're surrounded by buddies. You have friends, right? Hang with them. Or, sign up for an activity you dig (martial arts is great for kicking up confidence) and meet some other kids. Make a pact with pals to travel together in hallways or in the neighborhood.

6. It's OK to tell. Don't be ashamed to let an adult know how helpless you feel. You're not responsible for covering up a bully's behavior. Get counseling, if needed, to develop tools to deal with bullies.

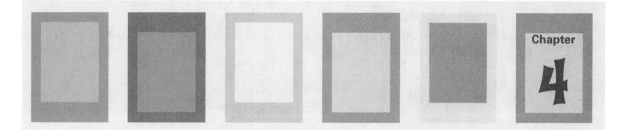

Tough Issues
Life Will Dish You

Tough Issues Life Will Dish You

No matter how grounded you are in feeling self-worth, you're going to be faced with occasional conflicts. You know—life's little challenges. But if you're like most girls, sometimes you might worry that your best is not quite good enough. Or how about the temptation to jump ship when stuff gets tough? Maybe you'll tell a little fib or indulge in a gossip session? Some challenges come about because, well, you made a less-than-admirable choice (you were poking fun of a friend behind her back, and she found out). Other challenges are completely out of your control (you haven't done anything to that girl in English class, but she continues to spread rumors about you).

The good news is that you can deal with these issues head on. So, without pulling your hair out, get a grip on the almost-certain self-esteem struggles that will inevitably come your way.

MISS PERFECT—NOT!

A few short years ago, the biggest challenge you might have faced was finding something edible in the cafeteria or picking out just the right tee. Now? Life is a race to keep up your grades, play sports, land the lead in the school play, volunteer at the animal shelter, and still have time to make the social scene. *Phew!* Tons of girls feel that talents like hitting homeruns, cracking hilarious jokes, playing a mean flute, or being a forever friend, just don't cut it anymore. Instead, girls feel like they have to be all-around superstars!

Do you feel you're expected to be the sweetest daughter, greatest friend, straight A student, top athlete, *and* music maestro? And don't forget about having cool clothes, clear skin, and social status.

If this is you, you are working way, way, way overtime to measure up to an unrealistic standard. More and more girls are setting themselves up for impossible goals—and then feeling like total failures, rather than realizing their wonderful worth. What's up with that?

Parental Pressure

Says Rachel, 12, "My mom thinks her job is to schedule every minute of my life. If I don't make daily progress toward at least one goal, she gets on me." Rachel is just one of many girls who say their parents over-manage their lives. Why do parents do this? Sure, they want the best for you. But sometimes it seems all about wanting you to be "brag-worthy."

"I think my mom gets a thrill from telling people I play No. 1 tennis singles and that I'm on high honor roll," Rachel says. "I swear it matters more to her than it does to me!" When you're doing well, your parents feel like they're doing a good job raising you. If you mess up, they feel like they've gone wrong somewhere, somehow.

Your Own Worst Enemy?

Perhaps your parents aren't the problem. Maybe you are putting the pressure on yourself! Once you break the school record for butterfly, you might think, "Yeah, but it's not the state record!" At what point will you feel your accomplishments are worth being proud of?

Since success is never guaranteed, it's best to take pride in how hard you tried and appreciate your efforts! But then the question becomes, "How do I know when I've done my very best?" Does trying your best mean getting to ice skating lessons on time, or does it require waking up at 5 a.m. every weekend to ace your axel?

It might be time to talk over your goals with your coaches, teachers, counselors, or parents. They can help you figure out what's appropriate.

They could also shed light on why you might not be getting the results you want despite your best efforts—and whether or not it might be time to change your focus.

The Downside to Overdoing

While hard work and determination are important to achieving any goal, there is also such a thing as overdoing it. And overdoing it can be downright destructive. Why? First off, it's exhausting to strive for perfection. Working three times as hard to get your tennis swing just right drains your energy for pursuing other important stuff. Staying up 'til midnight working on that extra credit science project robs your bod of restorative sleep. And you could readily develop stress-related disorders, such as headaches, stomachaches, fatigue, or recurrent colds.

That starts a vicious cycle. You feel like a failure, you give up trying and, then, your worst fears come true—you actually start to fail! By expecting perfection from yourself, you could be charting a hazardous course.

Put It in Perspective

Before perfectionistic pressure gets a stranglehold on you, alter your outlook. Forget the flaws. Focus on your strengths, not your weaknesses. Realize that reaching superstar status is utterly unrealistic. There are not enough hours in a day to accomplish everything.

It's nearly impossible to be at the top of the class, student government vice prez, and the school track queen. Can you do all this and also attend school, eat, bathe, clean your room, and sleep? Timewise, who could pull it all off? OK, some people seem to be able to pull off the impossible, but are they for real?

Wave the White Flag

While we aren't suggesting you come to a complete halt, it could be time for you to hop off that treadmill that's taking you on a fast trip to nowhere. Send an SOS to coaches, teachers, parents and friends: "I'm only one person. I can't live up to all these crazy expectations."

The key to all this? Balance! Reasonably divide your time between schoolwork, play time, hobbies, and healthy relationships with your buds and family. Drop that art appreciation class you don't really appreciate. Only sign up for soccer if you love the sport. Above all, laugh at your own goofs (everyone has them), and revel in your individuality.

To Lie or Not to Lie

O K, here's a really sticky situation for you: You tear through the door after day camp—only to be greeted by your mom's evil eye. Talk about pressure. "What's wrong?" you ask, scanning your brain to determine what your mom is about to unleash. Silently, your mom retrieves two ticket stubs from her pocket and holds them mere centimeters from your nose—as though you might have forgotten about that R-rated movie you and your BFF attended...without permission.

From time to time, your integrity will be put to the test with parents, friends, coaches, or teachers. And you'll be in the same sticky predicament—whether to tell the truth or tell a lie. It's your choice. We can't tell you what to do, but we can give you the low-down on lying.

Pants on Fire

"Uh-oh," you think, "I'm busted." Instantly, your heart contracts and that tell-tale "I'm guilty" shade of pink creeps into your cheeks. It's pretty impossible to explain away hard evidence. Your mom is now staring at you, as if to say, "Well?" Your head is spinning almost as fast as the washing machine, and you have to think fast.

You basically have three choices:

1) 'Fess up the truth.

2) Make up a story, any story.

3) Try to distract your mom ("Do you smell something burning?").

Two weeks ago, you had a fleeting thought about getting caught when you went to the flick, but you figured by now you were in the clear. Maybe you reassured yourself with thoughts like, "My mom will never find out," or, "She'll just say 'no,' so why bother asking to go?"

Often, you're tempted to lie to save your own skin or to get what you want. The following "benefits" of fibbing can sometimes make honesty seem like a really lame policy:

1. **Not being blamed.** Sometimes, lying seems to pay off. While truthful sorts seem to suffer, first-rate liars often get the goods. Alana, 10, says, "A bunch of us were in the girls bathroom, drawing on the wall, when a teacher caught us. I admitted to it and got detention. But some of my friends swore they didn't do it and got off scot-free."

2. **Avoiding problems.** Patrice, 11, once faked being sick because she forgot about a huge project due in art class, and called her mom to pick her up from school. She felt so guilty that she actually *did* feel sick that night! Later, after leaving a 'fess-up note on her mom's pillow, her illness was miraculously cured.

3. **Wishing it were true.** Sometimes you might say something you wish were true. Unfortunately, it's not, and that makes it a lie. For example, telling your father, "I finished all of my homework earlier." You would *prefer* that your English paper and math problems were done so you could go on-line with your friends. So maybe you're hoping that if you *say* this more pleasant thought out loud, it'll come true. Too bad that doesn't work!

4. **Impressing someone.** OK, like you've never been tempted to say something just to sound cool? Kris, 11, confesses that when she told her buds she was "e-mailing back and forth 24/7" with the cute boy from the rec center, it was kind of

an exaggeration (as in, the only time she actually spoke to him was in her dreams). Lots of girls lay it on thick in the quest to impress.

5. **Insecurity.** Some kids lie to cover up stuff that makes them uneasy or embarrassed. Say you're not exactly beaming with pride over your home-sweet-home (it's small or messy or needs fixing up). So when your bud suggests listening to CDs at your place, you say, "Nuh-uh. My mom's in bed with a contagious illness." Consider the possibility, instead, of trusting your friend to take the truth in stride.

6. **Avoiding conflicts.** Are you generally honest, except when you deal with a certain teacher, parent, or a difficult friend? If so, you might be dodging conflict in a relationship. Say your BFF always borrows your best clothes but takes forever to return them. So next time she hits you up for a skirt on loaner, you lie and say: "It's in the wash."

7. **Privacy.** Sometimes, a lie can come up like a major shield to protect your privacy. When someone asks if you're crushing on the new kid (you are), it's like your lips are set on automatic—"No way!"

The Liabilities of Lies

With all these temptations to twist the truth, what could possibly entice you to lay off the lying? Well, believe it or not, there are lots of really, really good reasons to curb the baloney cycle:

1. **Your conscience.** Remember the values your parents and teachers taught you? Now, personal ethics tell you lying's bad. And the guilt can gnaw at you pretty bad. Since you want to be a good person (right?), you should treat people the way you'd like to be treated. Ask yourself, "If the tables were turned, how would I feel if someone were dishonest with me?"

2. **Lying is habit-forming.** As Amanda, 12, says, "Once you start, it's hard to stop." The first one you get away with makes the next one that much easier. Some liars backpedal after letting one slip, and try to cover up by giggling and adding, "Oh, I'm only kidding!" But it's usually obvious when someone's trying to wriggle out of a fib.

3. **Lying consumes tons of energy.** Being a stellar liar takes work. You're juggling stuff all the time— what you said to whom and when. As Clara, 10, says, "I can never think fast enough when I try to lie. I get so confused that there's

absolutely no way I can do it right." Is lying really something you want to get good at? Your energy would be better spent reading a book, practicing the piano, or perfecting your jump shot.

4. **Lying creates off-the-chart tension.** Once you tell a lie, you often have to make up others to keep the first one going. You worry constantly about someone finding out. Can you keep your story straight, or will you trip up? Could your parents call other parents? Lisa and her friend Mariah, both 10, cooked up a scheme to tell their parents that they were going to the library, but they really were going to a skate park. Lisa says, "Every time my Mom asked a question about the plans, I felt like I'd throw up. I was a nervous wreck." Is this level of stress truly worth it? And consider what might happen if you're found out.

5. **Lying hurts people.** When people find out that you lied about some-thing, which is usually inevitable, they feel totally betrayed. Abby, 11, went bowling with her best friend's crush: "I told her I was going bowling with somebody, but I didn't say his name. When Meg found out, she went ballistic." When you "protect" your friend from the truth, rather than show her you care, your lie conveys

disrespect. Consider being up front from the start.

6. **Lying hurts you more.** Lies almost always come back to haunt you. Eventually, they make your problems worse. Going back to the R-rated movie fiasco—when you saw your mom holding those ticket stubs. If you tell more lies, you'll dig yourself a deeper hole. Even if you apologize profusely, chances are you won't be going to any sleepovers anytime soon. How can your folks trust you? You've screwed up your credibility. It stinks when people lose faith in you.

7. **Lying jeopardizes relationships.** Your folks might ground you for

When People Lie to You

Everybody agrees on one thing: Chronic liars are *sooooo* annoying! How to cope with a total fibber? For starters, you can tell the truth: "I really like you, but it's upsetting when you make stuff up." You might have to tell your friend it's hard to trust her or know when to believe her. A simple, "I'd much rather hear the truth," might do the trick. There's no question— girls who lie to your face, talk behind your back, or otherwise cause you to second-guess the friendship get tiresome pretty fast. Definitely do not confide your deepest, darkest secrets to an untruthful bud. If the lying continues, you might want to find new friends who say it like it is. You might not always like what truthful people have to say, but at least you know where you stand with them.

lying, but we doubt they'll say, "*Adios!*" Your amigas are another story. Telling a huge, hurtful lie can end a long and terrific friendship. Lucia, 11, found this out when trying out for a school play: "For weeks, I stressed to my friend Liz about how petrified I was that I wouldn't get the part. Liz kept saying she wasn't trying out. The cast list was posted, and my heart dropped when I saw her name. Liz got the part I wanted!" Not only was Lucia furious, but she also felt foolish. She says, "I trusted Liz with my fear. She obviously didn't see our friendship the way I did."

Take a Minute

Even if you try to be completely honest, an occasional lie will likely slip from your lips. You're human. Maybe you intend to come clean but chicken out. Or you just plain panic. But next time you're confronted with a direct question, you *do* have a choice: to lie or not to lie. If you feel panicky, buy some time instead of blurting out a blatant fib. Say, "I want to talk about this as soon as I put down my backpack." What you gain in honesty is the satisfaction of being real. Even if it hurts a bit, most people prefer the real thing over what's fake.

The thing is, once a lie is told, it's out there. Like a horrendous comment, it's nearly impossible to take back. So think long and hard before you decide whether to take the path toward truth or untruth. It's up to you. Just don't complain if your nose starts growing longer!

RUMOR MILL CENTRAL

Imagine this: You just saw Lori, the class brain, pull out a piece of paper during a spelling quiz. Miss All A's is a cheater! You can't wait to tell your best friend. After all, this is one rumor that's based on fact, not fiction. So it's not like you're spreading lies, right?

But here's the part of the story that you were missing: Lori was pulling some paper out of her pocket because she forgot to spit out her gum before class started. And that, girls, is how rumors get started. While most of us know better than to repeat nasty news, who can help it? No one, it seems. But should you keep your lips zipped? What happens when gossip hurts? Or worse, when the mean talk turns against you?

The Dirt on Gossip

Gossip is pretty impossible to avoid. Sit at the lunch table with your buds, and chances are that most of the caf chat is gossip. Gossiping is a natural way of communicating with your peers, and can be harmless and fun.

Gossip also supports your human need to bond with your buds and make clear who is in and who is out of the group. "It's pretty clear," says Constance, 12. "If you are in the clique, you hear what's going on. And you can be a tighter part of the clique if you have news to share." In other words, gossip—like knowledge—is power. And, because of that, it should be used carefully.

It's crucial to realize that constant gabbing and spreading of false rumors can backfire. People can get hurt, friends can become enemies, and reps can be tarnished by bogus gossip. Because everyone wants to be in on the talk, gossip can also lead to lying. Even people who usually don't lie might find themselves adding just a bit to a story. Says Debbie, "Back in my days as the town crier, I would put a little spin on things. Like, instead of people just getting caught skipping school, I would say they got caught by the

principal. I don't know why. I guess it just made for a better story. I didn't even really think of it as lying. Now I know better."

Clearly, gossip can result in some really bad consequences. So why do people do it so much? Again, it makes you feel part of the group. It's fun to be able to share something at the lunch table, especially something exciting that not everyone else knows about. And being able to make judgments about someone can also feel exciting and powerful. But gossiping can also be incredibly hurtful and unjust.

Gossip Consciousness

Remember, there's a difference between news and gossip. And even when gossip is true, it can be hurtful. Here are some good questions to ask yourself before sharing gossip:

✿ "Would I say this to the person's face?"

✿ "What would I think if someone said this about me?"

✿ "Why is it that I feel the need to tell this to people?"

Sometimes things just slip out of your mouth, but realize that spreading gossip can come at a price. The worst possible result of gossiping could be the loss of a friend's trust when she finds out you blabbed. Worth it? Didn't think so!

When the Talk Turns to You!

Sooner or later, *you* could become the hot topic of conversation. While some people don't mind the spotlight, others just want people to mind their own business. Here's some advice on how to handle it when your life practically becomes front-page news in the school paper:

✿ **Don't wig out.** The worst thing you can do is freak out. People don't always believe what they hear, and the story might not be as bad as you think. Try the casual approach. If the scoop isn't too bad, just try to laugh it off. Or wait until it comes up in conversation, briefly clarify if need be, and let that be the end of it. Try not to sound defensive, and don't attack back.

✿ **Find out what is going on.** Find a friend who knows the story that has been passed around, and ask her exactly what is being said. That way you'll know precisely what you're dealing with.

✿ **If the story is true.** It might be best to face it head on. If your parents are getting divorced but you wanted to keep the details hush-hush for now, tell your friends that. You aren't denying what is being said— you're just telling people you don't want them talking about the issue.

✿ *If the story is false.* You can do one of two things. You can rely on a friend to stick up for you. But that can get tricky. It takes guts to stand up for someone else—especially someone who is in the hot seat. Plus, it's not necessarily someone else's responsibility to get involved. Or, you can try sticking up for your- self. Sounds impossible, we know,

particularly when you already feel beaten down. But by being firm and cool, you can silence the masses. It takes guts, but the fallout from telling the truth might be better than the rumor.

✿ *Move on.* Once you say what you have to say, let the whole thing blow over. It might not seem like it when you're in the throes of a gossip storm, but these things often pass as quickly as the wind changes direction. Try to ignore the gossip-mongers, and remember that tomorrow is a brand new day!

QUIZ
Groovy Gossip Gauge

Sure, you know what everyone in your grade got on the English test, and you're the first to spill the news about a breakup. But that doesn't make you a gossip...does it? Nobody says you've got to keep your lips totally zipped. But could your motor mouth be running on overdrive? Take this quiz to find out.

1. You overhear Hannah from your homeroom tell the guidance counselor about how often her folks have been fighting. She's way upset. Would you tell your buds?

   a. No. You don't really know Hannah, and it'd be creepy to spread her bad news.

   b. Well...maybe you'd tell your closest girls and swear them to secrecy.

   c. Sure. Good dirt is good dirt.

   d. Why would you be even remotely interested in invading Hannah's privacy?

2. Your locker is next to the teachers' lounge. You're stashing a book when you overhear your math teacher bragging that he's springing a killer pop quiz on your class tomorrow. You:

a. make sure to put your math notes in your backpack—you'll need to study hard tonight.

b. pass the word along to your best buds *only*, so they'll have an edge.

c. freak out and run through the halls warning every classmate you see.

d. resolve to do your best on the quiz. You're not going to cram, and you're not going to tell anyone either. It would defeat the point of a pop quiz.

3. Psst...can you be trusted with a secret?

a. You're *so* not into secrets. You'd rather not even hear them in the first place.

b. Sometimes. If it's a really close bud's secret, you can totally keep it to yourself.

c. No. You've tried, but you just can't keep your big mouth shut.

d. You bet. You pride yourself on keeping all secrets securely under your cap.

4. How much do you know about the crucial topic of the "crush roster"?

a. A little.

b. Quite a bit.

c. A ton.

d. Crush *what*?

5. You're home alone when the phone rings. The machine picks up before you can get to it. It's your parents' accountant, talking about their finances. You and your sister have always wondered how much money your dad makes. Do you listen to the call?

a. Nope. Your 'rents wouldn't want you to have that info in a zillion years, so you zap down the volume.

b. Yeah. But you keep the info to yourself and don't share it with your sis. Besides, it's your parents' fault for not springing for their own voicemail.

c. Of course. How else will you and your sis know how much money you have to split for college tuition?

d. Definitely not. It's not your cash, nor your biz.

6. One afternoon, you're picking up some shampoo at the drug store. You spy your friend Maria and this boy Adam from your science class near the magazine racks, holding hands! Do you tell anyone?

a. Not a chance. You don't want to get involved.

b. You might tell Maria that you saw her with Adam.

c. Of course, you tell the whole crew. Why not? This is BIG!

d. You're going to forget you ever saw anything.

7. Today, your gym teacher made everyone run an obstacle course. This geek Conrad got his foot caught in a tire, and when he tried to shake loose, he fell flat on his face. The class burst out laughing. Would you tell the kids on your bus what happened?

a. Why? Word has spread so fast already, kids three towns over know about it.

b. No, but you might chime in if it comes up.

c. Why not? It was only the funniest thing you've ever seen.

d. Are you kidding? That would be cruel.

8. You totally dig hanging with your bud Samantha, but she doesn't do herself justice with her baggy jeans, stringy hair, and chapped, no-gloss lips. You overheard some guys ragging on her appearance, and you want to help. So how do you approach Sam about a makeover?

a. At the mall, you casually ask her to hit Wet Seal with you instead of the food court.

b. You playfully powder some makeup on her forehead to see how she reacts.

c. You tell her straight up, "You need a major overhaul, so sit still while I redo your 'do."

d. You say nothing. Sam should be allowed to dress any old way she wants.

9. You receive a nasty e-mail chain letter with mean gossip about some popular girls you don't like. What do you do?

a. Read it once, feel kinda bad, and delete it.

b. Read it and send it to your BFF only.

c. Read it over and over, laughing like crazy, and forward it to your entire address book.

d. Stop reading after the second sentence and trash it.

10. Your friend Matt invites you over for pizza and basketball on the tube. His big sis Pam is the most popular high-school girl you know. As you all watch players slam-dunk, Pam scribbles in her diary. Then Matt's mom yells that Pam has a phone call, while Matt excuses himself for soda refills. You're alone with Pam's open diary! Do you sneak a peek?

a. Nope. Pam is so intimidating you can hardly look at her, let alone her diary.

b. No, because Matt might catch you.

c. Oh, yeah! You grab it and read—fast!

d. No. That'd be a total invasion of privacy.

Scoring

Now tally up how many of each letter you selected. Then match up the results with the following.

Zipped Lips

Mostly A's: Gossip just isn't your bag. It's not like you're isolated from the whole world or anything—you just prefer to mind your own biz. You'd much rather spend your energy focusing on the things that matter in your life, like maintaining good grades, acing piano, or training for cross-country. Why worry about what's going on in everybody else's world? But remember, conversations from which you can absorb other people's thoughts and opinions, plus express your own, can be really fun and help you learn and grow. Positive chitchat is good for the soul.

As long as the gabbing doesn't get ugly, it's fun to spill about such-and-such's new-and-improved makeover or listen to the nitty-gritty details of that slumber party you missed because you were sick. Don't lose out on major girl-bonding time.

Rumor Realist

Mostly B's: OK, you're the first to admit it—when it comes to dish, you're only human. Sure, your ears perk up when you catch word of a meaty morsel of information. But, the cool thing about you is that you're sympathetic when it comes to gossip. Even being the style critic that you are, you wouldn't rip on the girl who sits behind you in homeroom if she came in one morning with a really bad perm. She probably feels bad enough about it already. Causing real pain to another person is the last thing you want to do.

But being a rumor realist means you totally understand why gossip can be so irresistible at times. It also means you're truthful about the consequences harsh gossip can bring and that you respect other people's feelings. Your empathy is admirable, so remember to keep zipping the lips when necessary.

Big-Time Busybody

Mostly C's: Oh, girl. Are you ever up in other people's business! You love talking dirt—who likes what boy...who failed what exam...who is wearing the worst outfit ever. If it's goin' on, you're on it! But you've been caught passing off your wild assumptions as cold, hard facts. Check the source? Who has time? If you don't spread the word, the news could be cold by Tuesday—and a girl's got to stay on top of things.

Though you'd probably be a fantastic asset to the *Neighborhood Tattler*'s editorial staff, you need to downshift that motor mouth. A little gossip is OK, and everyone has blabbed a rumor or two. But your obsession with gossip could mean trouble. Not only will people not trust, confide in, or believe you—they might even ditch you. Since you love the spotlight, why not audition for the school play instead of mocking the girls on your soccer team? From now on, vow to spread only good news.

My Way or the Highway

Mostly D's: You consider yourself to be above indulging in petty gossip, and your desire to avoid hurtful gab is admirable. Just be sure you don't come across with an air of superiority. In other words, there's no need to be the gossip police. If your friends want to gab about insignificant Hollywood rumors or other trite stuff, well, let 'em.

Also, remember that harmless gossip can be fun. So keep those ears perked, and feel free to let a juicy little morsel roll off the tip of your tongue. You *can* learn to love the power of positive dish! It's the gift of gab.

HELP! WHEN EVERYDAY SITCHES GET STICKY

Ever had a moment when you knew you'd messed up? It's OK—everyone has. And since life doesn't come with take-backs, we're here to help you out with some sticky situations.

Everyday Sitch:
Caught in the Act

You love your pals, you really do, but one of your friends has this annoying habit of TALKINGREALLYFAST—AND LOUD. You're doing your dead-on imitation of her, making your friends keel over, hysterical with laughter...

Turns Sticky:

...when your fast-talkin' girlfriend walks in. She witnesses the whole thing.

Problem Solved:

The truth is, lots of us have mocked even our best friends at one time or another. It's inevitable that the more time you spend with someone, the more you'll discover her quirky (and sometimes annoying) habits. But that doesn't grant you license to bash her—especially before an audience. Say your friends—the girls who are supposed to love you no matter what—were making fun of how you say "wash." You always stick an "r" sound between the "a" and the "s"— you can't help it. If your BFF were mocking you and sticking an "r" in the center of every other word, you'd be bummed, right? So, you have no choice...

Serve up a sincere apology—in front of your audience. Good friends will likely follow suit, and an honest group apology should ease the sting. But, the blatant bust also warrants a second apology—in private. Consider slipping her a "sorry" note. Remind her how much you care—a little groveling can't hurt. And the next time you want to get a laugh out of your crew, recite a joke you just heard instead—and spare your friend's feelings.

Everyday Sitch:
Breakin' the No-Boy Rule

You're hanging out with your boyfriend at your house. The two of you are watching TV...

Turns Sticky:

...when your dad walks in. You "forgot" all about that no-boys-in-the-house-without-adult-supervision rule.

Problem Solved:

Busted! No doubt, your parents are peeved. You're *definitely* in for the dreaded "We are so disappointed in you!" talk. The more mature you are about taking the tongue-lashing and inevitable grounding, the more likely your folks will be to go (somewhat) easy on you. You know you were wrong, so tell them. Say that you made a mistake and that you won't do it again, and mean it! Don't waste their time concocting some stupid story—your bikes weren't stolen and you weren't waiting for his mom to take you to the library. So, save it.

We can't guarantee you'll get to keep your TV privileges for next week, but hopefully your parents will see it as an isolated incident. Trust is the big issue here. If your 'rents see this as calculated disregard for their rules, they'll be less likely to trust you in the future. So show your folks that you're a trustworthy gal!

Everyday Sitch:
Camp Cold Shoulder

Like every summer, you head off to camp for six weeks of fun with your friends. The weather's great...

Turns Sticky:

...but, three days into camp, none of your buds will talk to you—and you have no idea why.

Problem Solved:

Unfortunately, fickle friends are a fact of life. Don't panic. Even if you dread

approaching their icy glares, you've gotta do it. If you're totally in the dark about why you're getting the brush-off, ask the girls what's up. Did you inadvertently hurt someone's feelings? Is there some other misunderstanding you're unaware of?

If they spill that it's over something silly, then apologize—hopefully, everyone can move on. If no one budges and you sense something more intense, you can't really apologize for something you're not sure that you did. Could be that you did absolutely nothing—perhaps your name just got dragged through the mud in some gossipy game. Get to the bottom of the mess if you can, and clear your name.

If your attempts to reconcile are ignored, or they can't come up with any real reason for the diss, then it's time to rethink your "friendships." Resist the overwhelming urge to make a scene, scream, shout nasty names, or spread vicious rumors. Going with a gag order is much more dignified. If other girls ask what's going down, politely tell them you'd rather not talk about it, and go forth with making new campfire friends. Don't mope, and don't let your "friends" see you being miserable. Girls in cliques often enjoy seeing their torture treatments pay off. Don't give them the satisfaction!

Everyday Sitch:
Tag Along Toddler

You planned a day at the amusement park to check out the new awesome coaster Killer Kolossus Vomitus with your buds...

Turns Sticky:

...but your mom says you have to bring along your little bro—who doesn't even come close to being ride regulation height.

Problem Solved:

Ah, the joys of being an older sister— a lifetime of free baby-sitting for your folks. Ask your mom if your brother can bring a buddy. It might seem like double the baby-sitting, but your bro and his friend will keep each other busy (and out of your hair). He'll have a partner for the kiddie rides and will be less likely to bug your friends. Politely hit your mom up for some extra dough for the day—you know, for some corn dogs to keep the little duo content.

As for checking out that great new coaster, stay on the sidelines with the little ones while your friends go on the ride. After they've had their fun (or lost their lunch), get your BFF to watch the munchkins while you and another bud go on the ride of your life. Then tell your fab (watchful) friend that the funnel cake is on you.

Everyday Sitch:
Damaging 'Do

You go to a chi-chi salon for a dramatic new look, and you tell the stylist you want a stylish shoulder-length look...

Turns Sticky:

...except she goes scissor happy and cuts your hair into a pixie 'do.

Problem Solved:

If you're itching for a totally new look, always bring a picture to the salon of exactly what you want. The stylist will be glad you did—and so will you. But, oops! Too late. You suddenly feel a sudden light breeze on the back of your neck. So now what?

You've gotta voice your disappointment to the hairdresser. Don't make a scene, but the hairdresser, owner, or manager needs to know you're not a satisfied customer. They probably won't ask you to pay for the cut. If they do, refuse payment and state your case—you asked for a specific cut. You weren't so specific? Pay up, and remember that pic next time.

Now, back to feeling better about your new cut. Maybe super-short hair wasn't what you had in mind, but make the best of it. Find pictures of celebs who look awesome in cropped 'dos, and copy those styles. There are lots of cute ways to sport short hair so you'll look like a princess. Tiny, shiny clips work, or go for a country look with a handkerchief tied over your hair. You'll look oh-so sassy.

Everyday Sitch:
Caught With the 'Rents

It's Friday night and you don't have any plans, so you go with the fam to see a movie...

Turns Sticky:

...when you spot your year-long crush, Blake, with all of his buddies. Do you duck behind the concession stand, or brave a hello and hope your parents don't say anything too embarrassing?

Problem Solved:

Newsflash: Blake probably has parents, too. This is a "get over it" situation. It's possible you could have just as easily run into Blake with *his* folks. Tell the 'rents you just spotted a friend and that you'll be right back. Dash off to say "hi," chat for a quick sec, and let him know you have to run. If you don't act all freaked about being seen with your parents, he won't either.

Still feeling a little uncool about the whole Friday-night-out-with-the-family thing? Remember, a night out with the 'rents means everything is on them. You've saved your baby-sitting money—and spotted your crush. All in all, not a terrible night.

Everyday Sitch:
Getting Gaudy Gifts

For your birthday, your BFF (who means well but has, um, different tastes than you do) buys you a gaudy shirt from the House of Rejects...

Turns Sticky:

...and you'd rather die than wear it.

Problem Solved:

Muster up a sincere "thank you." After all, she took the time to look for something she honestly thought you'd dig, and she spent her own cash on it. Gift giving can be tough, so give her a break.

Next, find a way to take the focus off the shirt, because you have to wear it in front of your friend—at least *once*. If possible, wear it under another shirt, with just the collar and cuffs showing. Or, team it with a great jacket to draw attention away from the weird blouse. Be careful not to let your true colors show by getting caught making fun of your BFF's questionable taste.

Everyday Sitch:
Missed By the Mail

The biggest bash of the year is going to be *so* cool, but it's invitation only...

Turns Sticky:

...and yours seems to have gotten lost in the mail.

Don't panic and immediately think that whoever is having the party hates you, or that you're not as cool as you thought you were. If the party is being thrown by one of your really close buds, then it's all right to ask, "Hey, Emily. I hear you're having a party." In which case, she'll probably say, "Didn't you get your invitation?" Problem solved.

If you're not so chummy with the party planner but think you should have made the guest list, get a friend who is invited to pal up to the hostess and do a little digging (you'll owe your friend for this one). Have her find out if it's an oversight or what. Brace yourself. Don't go into this one assuming your pal will come back with an invite in hand. If it didn't cross the party planner's mind to invite you, she didn't have enough invites, or whatever the story—you'll have to just accept it.

On party night, use the chance to hang with someone different. Give your quiet friend from soccer clinic a call. Do something you never do with your buds—race go-carts or play miniature golf. Hey, we can't all get invited to everything, but just think— that's one less person you'll have to invite to *your* next soirée.

You're hanging out in your backyard, and your crush walks by with his friends. He asks you to join him and the guys to play hoops...

...you want to hang out with him, but you don't want him to have a lasting image of you tripping over a big orange ball.

Guys love sporty girls. He'll probably think you're the coolest chick if you hop the fence and head to the court with the boys. Let the boys know up front that you're not so great but willing to give it your best shot. Challenge the guys to a game of Horse. You each take turns shooting the ball from a specific spot. Missed your shot? You get an "H." Made the next shot? Great! You're still in the game. Miss the next one, and you get an "O." Keep going until someone spells "horse." "Horses" are out of the game, but the others keep playing. You're not too bad of a shot, after all.

Work this to your advantage. Tell him you need help with your jump-shot. Suddenly, your sticky sitch has turned into a best-case encounter. Now, be careful not to drool when you dribble.

Future Success
Straight Ahead

Future Success Straight Ahead

It's time to put your rockin' self-esteem to work for you. Girl, that means get up and go, go, go! Where are you going? Toward your goals, of course! So get motivated, and give it your on-the-ball all. Even if you have to tweak and twist a tad to get positive results, that's OK. It takes a conscious effort to be your most wonderful you. So... what are you waiting for?

GO FOR GUTSY

Guts, gumption, verve, spunk. You've got to give it that extra oomph to truly achieve happiness and success. And guess what—you already have what it takes. "Hey, wait a sec," you might be thinking. "I'm really laid-back. My BFF is the one who'd have the nerve to bungee jump into the Grand Canyon. Just where is my spunk hiding—under that pile of dirty socks?"

Not exactly. That inner strength that powers you toward achievement is buried deep inside your personality. But it's up to you to build and develop it like a talent, so that you can eventually unleash it full-on. Think about being gutsy in the same way you'd learn to play a musical instrument. When you first pick up a flute, you have no idea how to play it or read sheet music. But you concentrate and practice, playing over and over again until you can master an entire song. You can rehearse being gutsy the same way—make courageous moves over and over until it feels totally natural.

Think about the vibrant, successful gals you look up to and admire, like your big sis or one of your favorite singers. It takes self-assurance and ambition to rise to the top. What can you learn from such amazing women? Check out the following traits they share.

❀ **They pay attention to the world around them to figure out how to go after their dreams.** Actresses, for example, have the ambition to go after good roles and develop their talent.

❀ **When faced with something scary—but at the same time totally worth trying—they try it.** Gutsy girls might feel fear at first, but they always find a way to beat it.

❀ **They give it their all.** Truly gutsy girls work long and hard to meet a goal. For you, that could mean perfecting your balance beam routine or rewriting that essay until your teacher can't deny its brilliance.

❀ **They don't let failure define who they are.** Your team won't win every game, either. So what? Gutsy girls weather little losses along the way. Why see one little failure as the end of the world? Instead, figure out what you can learn from the experience and try to change things the next time around.

❀ **They proceed with caution.** After all, we're not shooting for over-the-top self-confidence here. Who wants an ego so huge it could eat Chicago?

So how do you put your spunk into practice, and keep remaining wonderful, level-headed you? Here's how to navigate some tricky situations with strength and common sense.

Singin' in the Rain, Shakin' in Your Boots

You're dying to try out for your school's production of *Oklahoma*. But you've never sung in front of an audience before, and you're terrified beyond belief. How can you stir up the nerve to audition?

The Gutsy Girl Response: First, admit that you're scared. Everybody's scared of something. The trick is to break down your fear, bit by bit, until you understand it— because when you fully understand something, you calm down and let logic take over. Then you'll get that there's  nothing to freak over. The fear of performing in public is incredibly common. Even lots of famous actors and singers get stage fright.

Rehearsal is the road to Chillville. Choose a song you want to sing at your audition, and get it on CD. Every chance you get, lock yourself in your room and sing along to the CD. Do this until you feel so comfy with every note, you could sing the tune in your sleep. Then try belting it out in front of a full-length mirror. Smile, relax, stand up straight, and feel good about how you look while you're singing.

Once the song is etched into your vocal chords, choose someone you trust—like your mom—and sing it for her. Bet she'll give you a standing ovation. Next, ask a sibling to be your audience...then your BFF... and so on. Appreciate the positive encouragement. Their support is well-deserved. Now get out there and nail that audition.

See how you broke down your fear? You practiced doing the thing you feared, note by note until you were completely comfortable with it. Then you further proved you had nothing to fear by singing for others and letting them show you their approval. So rather than being frozen by fear, you outsmarted it.

Spunk Smarts: If you get a role in the school play, break a leg. If you don't, join your school's chorus, or look into private voice lessons. You might have a natural singing talent, but it takes time to fine-tune  a diva's voice. Consider your first audition a learning experience and throw your energy into practicing. Imagine what tip-top shape your voice will be in when auditions for *Grease* roll around!

Breaking the Ice

Say you really want to strike up a conversation with Josh from your homeroom. He smiles at you every morning as you walk to your desk which is directly behind his. Yet, he never utters a word. You *sooo* want to talk to him, but how?

The Gutsy Girl Response: There's nothing wrong with taking the initiative to talk to this boy. A shy guy will really appreciate that

you want to talk with him, and it will take a load off his shoulders. You can bet if Josh *does* like you, he's been racking his brain to come up with a clever way to spark a convo—imagine his relief when you give him a green light.

For a clear break, be observant. Check out the stuff on Josh's desk. Is he doing some homework before class? Take a peek at which subject he's tackling. If he's memorizing French vocab, ask him if he knows how to tell whether a noun is masculine or feminine. Be friendly, and give him a chance to respond. Don't get lost in his dark-brown eyes. Really listen to what he says to show him you're really interested.

Spunk Smarts: Taking the initiative is great, but it's not cool to be overly aggressive. Let things move along at a reasonable pace. If you two click during

an initial chat, talk with him again the next day. Don't force it. Crushes come and go.

Let's Make a Deal

In your opinion, your mom is being totally unfair about your curfew. On Friday nights, your crew always catches a movie. You have to be home by 8:30 p.m., an hour earlier than any of your friends. This means that sometimes you actually have to go home before the flick's even over. You feel like a total toddler as you trudge out of the theater to meet your mom in the parking lot. You really want to hammer out a new deal for a later curfew.

The Gutsy Girl Response: If you really feel you're mature enough to stay out later, then present your case in a mature manner. Don't go on and on about how uncool your mom is and how she treats you like a little kid. Explain to her that you can understand she's concerned  about your well-being. As hard as it is for some girls to believe, your mom is not out to make you look like a geek or to get you laughed at by the kids who get to stay out 'til 9:30.

That said, try and cut yourself a new deal. Say something like, "I know you want me to be safe, but I really can handle a later curfew. I'm responsible—look at how I brought up my algebra grade this semester. Do you think we could go for a 9:00 curfew, just on a trial basis—and if that works out, eventually up it to 9:30?" You're asking politely, showing your mom you're considerate of her feelings, and pointing out your sense of compromise and responsibility. She'll most likely take your request into consideration because you've presented your side in a solid, straightforward way—without whining.

Spunk Smarts: Slamming doors and complaining are *not* good tactics here. Being bratty does not equal gutsy. And flipping out won't get you anywhere but grounded. If your mom won't go for a later curfew, accept that she has to go with her own comfort level.

How Not to Choke

Even the gutsiest girl alive can encounter a case of anxiety from time to time. If you find yourself in a situation where you feel like you might choke, here's an easy solution:

- Mentally review all of your past successes. Relive times you did well until you feel cool, calm, and collected. It's a great idea to actually memorize a list of your accomplishments so you can refer to it whenever you need to.

- Boost your self-esteem by asking yourself what your role model would do if she were in a situation like yours—imagine how she might deliver your book report. Try standing or speaking in the same comfortable manner that she would.

- Most of all, be proud. Accept that things may not go your way all of the time—but always give it your best shot. That's what being a gutsy girl is really all about!

Be a BFF, Not a Boss

Your BFF is awesome. She's smart, funny, and kind to everyone. So when you have a heavy problem, you go to her. Just one thing—she's a motor mouth! She blabs your stuff to everybody. You wouldn't be surprised if she posted it on the Internet! You don't confront her because you don't want to create friction in an otherwise fine friendship.

The Gutsy Girl Response: You really care about your friendship, and that's admirable. But when something about your BFF affects you in a bad way, be brave and speak up. Explain to your so-called bud that you confide in her because you  trust her. As nicely as possible, break it to her that you won't be able to share secrets if she doesn't respect your confidence.

Spunk Smarts: There's a fine line between standing up to your bud and bossing her around. Telling her she should cut her bangs, improve her posture, study harder, or eat less between meals is not your job. In fact, it's none of your business. Why not? 'Cause it doesn't affect you.

Being bossy shows insecurity, not gutsiness. Offering advice that your BFF doesn't want will just drive you apart. You guys are super close, but your bud has her own free will. Being secure with yourself means you don't need to control another person's likes, dislikes, or behavior. It means you're strong enough to be the best person you can possibly be and let your friend do  the same. What if a friend asks you for help? Well, in that case, of course, dole out the advice—but still be kind! What are friends for, right?

QUIZ
Are You Game?

OK, you've memorized your guide to gutsy spunk, but does the thought of taking a stab at something you've *never* tried get you totally jazzed or seriously spazzed? Whiz through this quiz to gauge your get-up-and-go groove!

1. **The coolest girl just moved to town from Morocco, and she invites you over to dinner. The food smells fantastic but looks completely weird. You:**

   a. dig in. You love trying funky, far-out foods.

   b. try a bite to be polite, and pray you don't hurl.

   c. fill up on bread and salad, and create a couscous sculpture.

2. **You've always had long hair, but lately you're really loving some of the shorter styles you've seen on other girls. At your next salon appointment, you'll probably:**

   a. get up the nerve to go pure pixie!

   b. go for something a little shorter but still long enough to pull into a ponytail.

   c. freak if your hairdresser dares to cut off more than a fraction of an inch.

3. **As a fun present, your parents give you a pair of sneaker skates. Your reaction?**

   a. Lame! Real in-line skates are the only way to travel.

   b. Cool! Sneaker skates are a fun new fad for your feetsies.

   c. Confusion! The skates are kinda cool, but your folks know you never even mastered those plastic skates they got you when you were five.

4. **The vacation of your dreams would include:**

   a. visiting a foreign country. You'd love to explore an exotic land.

   b. tagging along with your BFF on her family's annual ski getaway.

   c. camping at a nearby lake with a few of your closest friends.

5. **You have to pick 10 books from the library's read-a-thon list. You:**

a. pick all the books you've never heard of—especially those real-life adventure stories like the ones about climbing Mt. Everest.

b. ask the librarian to suggest a few can't-miss classics, and then you choose the rest from the science fiction section (your fave).

c. choose from your older sister's collection. You two don't always have the same taste, but at least you know what you're getting.

6. **You've decided to sign up for an extracurricular activity. By next week, you'll be:**

a. on the archery range! It's not the most practical sport, but when else will you ever get a chance to shoot a bow and arrow?

b. trying out for the musical. Performing in front of a big audience is new to you, but you were in your school's talent show last year and loved being in the spotlight.

c. doing crafts. Art is your favorite subject at school, so why not?

7. **Imagine winning a $200 gift certificate to a clothing store of your choice. You'd pick:**

a. some funky boutique that carries everything from vintage to designer.

b. a huge department store with tons of different styles.

c. someplace safe and familiar that's not particularly snazzy.

8. **Your community center is offering diving lessons—something you've always wanted to try, but never had the guts. You:**

a. sign up and get psyched by watching some diving competitions on cable. That could be you one day!

b. call the instructor to see if you can go to the first lesson on a trial basis and make a decision after that.

c. pass. What happens if you belly-flop in front of everyone?

9. **A guy you've had a crush on asks if you want to go for a snack after school—just the two of you. You:**

a. let him plan everything—you love surprises!

b. pick your favorite burger joint, but let him order for you.

c. suggest grabbing some chili-cheese fries at the '50s-style diner, where most of your friends hang out.

10. **After you help your dad with a ton of chores around the house, he offers to take you out to do anything you want over the weekend. You choose:**

a. going out to lunch for sushi (you've been dying to find out what all this raw fish rage is about).

b. a golf outing because you've always wondered if golf is extremely cool or painfully boring.

c. tickets to a community theater production of *Romeo and Juliet* since you see it every year. It's tradition.

Now, review your answers and determine the letter you chose most often. Then, read below to see what that means about you.

"Count me in!"

Mostly A's: If someone invited you to swim with sharks or offered you *escargot* (that's French for "snails"), you'd probably say, "Sure thing!" You're always up for just about anything. Life is way too short to shy away from new things simply because you've never tried them before. Heck, once upon a time, you had never listened to reggae music either, but now you love it.

Besides, how are you ever going to become a champion surfing diva if you can't handle a few falls? Keep seeking out new experiences—it's the absolute best way to learn about new cultures, interesting people, and even yourself. Trying new stuff makes you a more rounded, more interesting, and more confident you. As long as you play it safe and smart, you're on the right track. Keep it up!

"Let me check my calendar."

Mostly B's: Sometimes you're a real adventurer, and other times you play it safe. With a little encouragement, you're willing to try new ideas and experiences—but only if they aren't completely crazy. So next time someone invites you to try something that appeals to you even the teensiest bit, like eating Indian tandoori chicken or playing Ultimate Frisbee, just go for it.

Trying new things can be a gamble, but it's worth the risk if it turns you on to a new favorite munchie or sport. When opportunities present themselves, remember to let your guard down every once in a while—you'll be glad you did.

"I don't *think* so."

Mostly C's: OK, just because something is new to you doesn't mean it's scary, lame, or bad. And just because you normally do things one way doesn't mean another way is wrong—just different. True, it's hard to stomach the idea of being a beginner at tennis when you're already a soccer pro. But if you don't try new stuff, you could miss out—big time.

If nothing else, trying new things gives you a better idea of your own preferences. That way when someone offers you *caviar*, you can honestly say, "No, thanks. I've tried it before, but it's not my thing." So branch out every now and then—bet you'll be surprised to discover all the things you've been missing!

SAY GOODBYE TO BEING SHY

Maybe you have a hard time mustering up your inner spunk because you're shy. You'd just as soon pass up the party of the century than have to walk into a crowded room? Get out your party dress. No matter what degree of shyness you suffer from, you can trade in coy for joy.

Whether you're going to your best bud's b-day party or your mom is dragging you to Aunt Gertrude's for tea, odds are you'll have to strike up a conversation with someone. Your alternative is to sit in the corner all evening keeping company with the punch bowl. Welcome to wallflower hour!

You can barricade yourself in your bedroom and become known as a first-rate recluse if you want. But what follows is some great bashful-bashing advice that's sure to help you get through your next social outing and beyond.

Shy-busting Solutions

Learn to be a social butterfly instead of having butterflies in your stomach. Whether you're terminally shy or just shy on occasion, here are some tips for tackling the timids.

🌼 **Quit focusing on yourself.** Shyness is often about self-consciousness. Suddenly, you're convinced that every blink of your eye or twitch of your nose is obvious to everyone around you. Forget about it. Nobody (but you) is analyzing your every move. And so what if you make a few goofs? You're probably the only person to notice anyway— or care.

🌼 **Fake it.** Tap your inner drama queen. Before going to any gathering, practice chatting it up in front of your bedroom mirror. Make a mental list of three topics you can bring up so you'll have something to contribute to the conversation once you get there. And don't forget to breathe. Don't take quick, shallow breaths. Slowly inhale through your nose and exhale through your mouth.

🌼 **Be a good listener.** A good way to strike up a conversation with someone is to show a sincere interest in her life by asking about her hobbies, family, pets, and so on. She just might take the conversation from there, and your silence can be golden. Sometimes it's good simply to listen. Pay attention to what is being said, and interject a few verbal cues— "Yes," "Uh-huh," "Really?"—to let her know you're hanging on her every word.

🌼 **Keep the conversation on a two-way street.** Try not to get nervous and babble non-stop. That's not a conversation—it's a monologue. A conversation is back-and-forth banter. She's telling you about her piano lessons? When she pauses, tell her you play guitar. Then listen while she tells you about that concert she just went to, and so on.

🌼 **Know when to quit.** No matter how hard you try, some conversations will be duds. Look for visual cues that your listener is bored. (Or maybe you're bored.) If he is looking around, tapping his foot, sighing, or showing other signs of restlessness, give it up. Dismiss yourself with something like, "Well, I think I'll go over and try the Jell-O mold." Stop thinking about how you blew it—it might be that the other person was just as nervous as you were.

✿ *Keep working on it*. Now that you've made it through the dance, don't be so quick to go back to your bashful ways. Instead of focusing on how nervous you are about attending next Saturday's party, relax by riding your bike, meditating, or starting a journal. Or, take up a sport or activity that will help you put your newfound social skills to the test. Your best friend is begging you to join French club with her? Great! You'll meet other kids, and who knows, *mon ami*. Next time around you could be the life of the party! *Non?*

SHAKE THOSE LABELS!

You can shake shyness and be as gutsy as can be, but another roadblock to great self-esteem is the problem of being labeled. Maybe you've become known as a "goody-goody," "flirt," "fake," "nerd," or "space cadet." But no matter how many times you've strived to shed the old image, it's managed to stick to you like a big, annoying "kick me" sign. Take note of the following tips, and you'll find out exactly how to replace your old image with the new, true you.

The Academic You

Perhaps your teacher has a pet name for you, like Sleepyhead, Chatterbox, or Grouchy. While these nicknames were humorous at first, they're played out. Being labeled can prevent you from seeing yourself as you really are. Sure, maybe you sometimes doze in class, talk too much, or scribble your homework—but these are not your all-defining qualities,

and these tags you've been given can really get in the way of your genuine persona.

Hinda, 9, knows what it's like to be labeled. Talking about a class with a particularly strict teacher, she says, "Sometimes I got scared and forgot what I was going to say. Then everybody started calling me 'Miss Clueless' and I hated that, so I'd get

even more nervous when I got called on, and my mind would go blank."

You're sick of your image and desperate to chuck it? It's time to plan a strategy. You have to decide how you want to be perceived, and figure out what it would take for you to be seen in that new way. To really change your academic rep, you might need to make changes not only in your study habits but also in your lifestyle.

Jill, 11, had been dozing off in morning classes, and by third period all she could think about was her growling stomach and the tater tots on the lunch menu. She decided she needed to take drastic measures: "Now, I make myself eat breakfast, even if I just wolf down a bagel," she says. "And I go to bed earlier—even though I hated it at first." Making lasting changes isn't easy. But once you've put your new behaviors into practice, you should be on your way to an improved image.

The Social You

For most girls, a top priority is how they're seen on the social scene. And sometimes it's tough to escape a bad rep that's haunted you since you made that one teensy mistake.

As Holly, 12, reports, "I was way too flirty with this guy at the spring dance, and after that everybody accused me of being boy-crazy." So how did she deal? "I kept a low profile for a while. Then I went out of my way to show everyone I had changed. I told my good friends what I was doing so they'd under-stand." Holly's plan worked because she truly *did* change her ways. It wasn't that Holly's changes were noticed automatically, but everyone seemed more open to recognizing her efforts.

Other girls are pigeonholed as the "jocks," "brains," "nerds," or whatever. Or maybe you've decided that no matter what it takes, you'll be one of the "cool" girls. This wish to be popular, to join the "A-list," is what lures many girls down mis-guided paths. Some get fanatical, buying new wardrobes or getting radical new 'dos to project an entirely different image. Having just moved to a new school, Sarah, 12, decided to go glam. "I got all these new clothes and a new hairdo," she says, "and some of the popular girls were nice to me, but most thought I was a huge poser—which I was. I ended up feeling dumb."

If you genuinely share interests or participate in common activities, getting to know others better will happen naturally. No matter how tempting, it's usually a bad idea to try to change your behavior, values, or whole self just to fit in with friends. Pay close attention to any and all uncomfortable feelings. They could be clues that getting a new image or reputation comes at too high a price.

The Real You

Some girls want to focus on changing their images at home, within their families and, most especially, with themselves. Somehow, without even understanding how it happened, you can end up seeing yourself as lazy, ditzy, forgetful, dishonest—you name it! But you're not stuck with those labels. You can change every one of them with a little effort.

Mary, 12, for example, was determined to change her reputation as the family slob. "I was sick of everyone calling me 'Miss Piggy'," she says. So she started with one area at a time, putting things in their proper places. "Every night, I straightened up a little more until, finally, I was pretty neat."

Sometimes, family members are the last to recognize changes you've worked so hard for. Once they've slapped you with a label, they might continue to see you in that same light—even if you've changed. You could have to bring them up to date.

Even tougher is making changes in how you see yourself. Lianne, 14, had always thought of herself as lazy. Eventually she figured out she was really just finding an excuse to get out of doing chores and homework she disliked. "It's been hard to make myself do stuff," she says. "Sometimes it works, and sometimes it doesn't. But at least I'm trying."

Trying counts for a lot. Even if you're not immediately or totally successful, making the effort makes you feel better about who you are and what you are capable of accomplishing. It takes strength, courage, and commitment to try to change your behavior for the better—that, and some really hard work.

To make sure you succeed, keep your goals realistic, and be true to yourself. Best of all, enjoy your new changes. Once they're habit, they're yours—and no one can take them away from you. So good luck!

QUIZ
Face to Face with Your Fear!

Now that you're so together, wouldn't it be a shame to let your fears get in the way of your success? We're not talking about a fear of heights or being freaked out by bugs. What if you're scared of something a little harder to explain? Like, the mere thought of trying out for chorus makes you want to crawl under the covers and never come out.

Did you know you can have a fear of rejection? Or actually be scared of success? These are emotional fears, and they're different than being scared of the dark. Emotional fears can keep you from achieving things. Take this quiz to find out what could be putting the brakes on you being your absolute all. Go ahead—what are you afraid of?

1. **Sean, the cute boy who sits behind you in English, passes you a note inviting you to join him for pizza in the caf. You've only adored him from afar for the past three months! You immediately feel:**

   a. shy and dorky. You're totally freaked about eating in front of boys—especially Sean!

   b. suspicious. He's probably just kissing up to you because you rock at math, and he didn't finish his algebra homework or something.

   c. horrified. You're bound to blow it the second you speak.

   d. thrilled! But then you remember you should get to work on a book report that's due next month.

2. **Your tyrannical gym teacher announces that you'll be climbing a 10-foot rope. You hate the thought of this because:**

a. you hate physical stuff like sports! You always feel like a total klutz.

b. if you fall off that rope, you'll surely be the laughing stock of the entire grade.

c. there's no way you can possibly crawl even an inch up that thing, so why bother?

d. you train in gymnastics four days a week, so you'll be able to climb that thing in about two seconds flat. What's the big deal?

3. **Your godmother takes you on a mega shopping spree for your birthday. She pulls this totally cute spaghetti-strap tank dress off the rack and says how perfect it would look on you for the holiday dance. You try it on, and when you catch your reflection in the mirror, you think:**

a. "It looks pretty good...doesn't it? Or do my upper arms look a little flabby?"

b. "It looks OK. The light in here is kind of funky, though. I'll bet in broad daylight my stomach pooch will definitely show."

c. "It looks terrible. But, then again, everything looks terrible on me."

d. "It looks fantastic! If I wear it to this dance, though, I'll have to get my hair and makeup done, and then I'll need to have an even more amazing dress for the next dance. No way can I pull off looking that good twice in a row."

4. **Your buds are urging you to run for student council. They think you're smart and have a winning personality—and that you'll win in a landslide! What are you thinking?**

a. You're flattered, but you figure if they knew how mortified you'd be giving a campaign speech at an assembly, they wouldn't be so sure you'd win.

b. They're just buttering you up so you'll spring for fries on the next trip to the mall.

c. They've flipped. You'll get four votes (and that includes your own).

d. What if they're right? You just might win. But then, it's not like you'd have a clue what to do after that.

5. Your BFF from first grade moved away a few years ago. She recently got back in touch with you because she's coming back to her old neighborhood for a visit and wants to get together with you. You:

   a. actually feel nervous. You two were like sisters, but you haven't seen her in eons. What if she's spooked by your new goth look?

   b. worry that you two won't get along like you used to and you'll never hear from her again. Maybe you should just keep her strictly as a phone friend.

   c. feel happy she can fit you into her plans, but you wonder what made her even think of you.

   d. are thrilled and frantic all at the same time. You'd better think up some fun things for you two to do while she's here so she won't get bored.

6. Taylor has been your BFF since the third grade, but lately she's been acting kind of distant—like, bailing on trips to the movies and not calling when she says she will. What's running through your brain?

   a. You're convinced you'll be a loner any second now. You know she's totally about to dump you.

   b. You're not surprised. You never trusted her sugary-sweet smile, anyway.

   c. This proves you were never good enough for Taylor.

   d. Forget a fair-weather friend like that. But you're concerned you'll never be able to make a new BFF.

7. Your music teacher tells you he'd like you to audition for all-state chorus. How do you react to this big-time opportunity?

   a. Your stomach turns cartwheels at the mere thought of trying out—you'd have to sing a solo!

   b. You assume your teacher probably asked everyone in the entire class before asking you as a last resort.

   c. You're not interested! You'll never make the cut, so what's the point in auditioning?

   d. You're psyched! But you don't want to deal with the time commitment and the drag of having to find a ride after rehearsals.

8. **You arranged some flowers for your mom's surprise birthday party. One of her friends was totally impressed and wants you to do centerpieces for her next party—for money! You worry that:**

a. your mom's friend's style is really sophisticated. What if the arrangement you come up with isn't grown-up and tasteful enough?

b. she's just trying to be nice, giving you a fake compliment— no way does she really intend to hire you for her party.

c. you'll stink at it! Tossing some daisies in a vase for Mom is one thing, but a real, professional job like that? Forget about it!

d. you pulled it off once, but your flower power has its limits. What if *all* of your mom's friends start asking you to arrange their rose petals? That's a lot of pressure.

9. **You shatter the school record for the 100-yard butterfly! As you climb out of the pool to the sound of a cheering crowd, your brain keeps repeating, like a stuck CD:**

a. "Is my suit riding up?"

b. "They're just applauding to be polite."

c. "The time clock must be broken."

d. "Great, now I have to defend my record at the next swim meet."

10. **Who's the gutsiest chick in a flick?**

a. Alexa Vega in the *Spy Kids* movies. When she saves her mom and dad from those evil villains, she projects total confidence.

b. Emma Watson in the *Harry Potter* films. She's cool, collected, and thinks before she acts.

c. Anne Hathaway in *The Princess Diaries*. Her character is a geek who made good and stood up to the school bully.

d. Reese Witherspoon in *Legally Blonde*. She goes after her goals fearlessly.

Add up your points accordingly. Then, brave up and face your fear below!

1. (a) 4, (b) 3, (c) 2, (d) 1
2. (a) 2, (b) 4, (c) 3, (d) 1
3. (a) 4, (b) 3, (c) 2, (d) 1
4. (a) 4, (b) 1, (c) 2, (d) 3
5. (a) 3, (b) 2, (c) 4, (d) 1

6. (a) 2, (b) 3, (c) 1, (d) 4
7. (a) 4, (b) 2, (c) 3, (d) 1
8. (a) 4, (b) 1, (c) 3, (d) 2
9. (a) 4, (b) 3, (c) 2, (d) 1
10. (a) 1, (b) 3, (c) 2, (d) 4

Fear of Embarrassment

32 to 40 points: As you mature, it's normal to become self-conscious. You probably exaggerate and overanalyze every perceived flaw—and think the itsy-bitsy red bump that's sprouted on your forehead looks the size of a third eye. *Reality check:* Your so-called "flaws" are not nearly as bad as you think. Also, people around you do not obsess over your cowlick. Do you judge people on unimportant details? Doubt it! You're smart enough to know a bad hair day doesn't make for a bad person.

The good news is there's a lot you can do to shake the fear of embarrassment. First, don't beat yourself up for feeling embarrassed and don't measure yourself by anyone else's standards. Remind yourself of your great qualities daily, 'til you know you rule! If you like yourself and your inner voice tells you you're doing the right thing, you're on the right track.

Beat Your Fear: Changing your 'tude is terrific. But to really beat your fear, change your behavior. Desensitize yourself. Say you walk into the caf and there are no familiar faces. All your friends have a later lunch. Be independent! Break your fear by sitting alone the first day. Eye out people to sit with tomorrow. The next day, ask the new girl if she wants a lunch partner. You could have a new bud by sixth period.

Fear of Rejection

24 to 31 points: A fear of rejection is really a fear of risk. Anytime you put yourself out there—as a friend, girlfriend, or even a daughter—you face the possibility of rejection. Some people are so scared of being rejected, they won't take even the tiniest risk. *Reality check:* Terror at the thought of rejection proves how sensitive you are.

Look at it this way: If you stick your neck out and attempt to be friends with somebody who blows you off, who's the one who deserves to be rejected? You offered your kindness to someone who doesn't deserve it. Not everybody will accept you—that's life—but you've got to risk rejection to meet great people.

Beat Your Fear: Go back to that cutie Sean from English. If he asks you to eat lunch with him, do it and enjoy yourself! If you're suspicious of his motives, you probably feel you aren't worthy of his attention—but is that fair to Sean (or to you)? No way! So give him a chance to show what kind of guy he is.

If you're deeply distrustful of people and can't shake the belief that everyone will betray or leave you, figure out what's up. Are your folks at odds with each other? Have you gone through a really scary or traumatic experience? If so, don't be afraid to ask for help from a family member or counselor. You don't need to carry such a heavy weight—you *can* learn to trust other people.

Fear of Failure

17 to 23 points: You'd rather bow out than try something and fail. What's the deal with that? We're betting someone told you that you weren't good enough—and you believed it. Shake it off! What does someone else's negative and thoughtless opinion mean to you?

Successful people fail again and again until they achieve what they want. *Reality check:* Failure can put you on a path to success! You can't make progress until you try.

Beat Your Fear: Look at the times you feared you'd fail and didn't. How freaked were you beforehand? Then how did you feel when you made it through successfully? Relieved! Proud! Accomplished! See? You *earned* those feelings.

Fear of Success

10 to 16 points: Fear of success can be pretty intense and complicated because when you fear success, you do things to hold yourself back—stuff you might not even realize you're doing. On the surface, that sounds weird, because why would anybody be scared of doing well? Because of the pressures success can bring. Say you get elected class prez, and the first thought you have is, "Oh, no! What do I do now?" That's because you're afraid you won't live up to the expectations of other people—maybe your classmates and, likely, yourself.

People who fear success are usually perfectionists. They won't do anything unless they can do it perfectly and, therefore, they stall their own success. *Reality check:* Remember, few situations are perfect. Life isn't perfect. You aren't perfect. Nobody is. So you might as well get on with things and just do your best.

Beat Your Fear: Find someone who's successful—say, your drama teacher, who's been in many plays and can give you acting tips. Look to role models—parents, friends of parents—who are happy with themselves, striving, and hardworking.

If you're confronted with great results—say you're on a winning tennis streak—don't fret over whether you can keep pulling those rabbits out of your hat. Inspire yourself with a success story. If you're scared to do something but have pushed past your fear, you've proven that you think enough of yourself to go for greatness. That alone is true success!

31 THINGS YOU CAN DO BETTER

You're most likely to succeed and have super self-esteem if you put your mind to it. Read the following tips on how to be tops.

1. Take a better class picture.

Why does your BFF's class picture seem like a glamour shot but you look like you're on *America's Most Wanted*? A lot of people get nervous, and that's when pictures turn out looking goofiest. Relax, and wear a black shirt that doesn't have a high neckline. Yearbook photos are usually black-and-white, so the more contrast, the better. As for wearing any crazy prints, doing your hair differently, or wearing a lot of makeup—forget about it!

Remember to say, "Cheese!" and think positive thoughts about yourself.

2. Write a better essay.

Believe it or not, whipping up a stellar report isn't all about being a great writer. The research you do on your subject is what really matters. Go to the library, or browse the Web to look up facts—dates, names, and events related to your topic. Then, in your opening paragraph, clearly state the topic you're writing about: "Native Americans got a bum deal from Western settlers." Then back up that statement with the most interesting facts from your piles of research. Oh, and don't forget to use spellcheck.

3. Get a better report card.

How do you get better grades when it feels like you're already working your tail off? "Study one more hour a night," says straight A student Christy, 13. "More studying sounds awful, but when I added just one more hour a night to my homework time, I went from a few A's and some B's to all A's." Is it worth it? "You bet. Now I know I can do it."

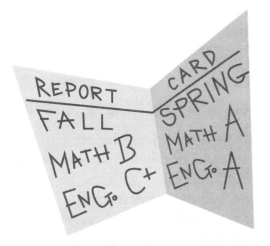

4. Have more guy friends.

To become one of the guys, simply treat them like you treat your girl buds—be nice, hang out,

have fun. If lack of exposure is the problem, throw a party with some friends and plan stuff that boys like as much as girls, such as playing a big game of softball. (Whatever you do, don't talk about who likes who. Just a hint.)

5. Grow an inch instantly.

Newsflash: Standing up straight makes you feel better, look better, and exude unshakeable confidence. Stand with your weight centered on both feet, and gently pull your shoulders back and down. Then, pull your neck back and up so your head is centered between your shoulders, and slightly lift your chin. Inhale, lifting your chest, and exhale, through your mouth, without dropping your head. Hey, how's the weather up there?

6. Tell a scarier ghost story.

Spin a good scary tale at your next slumber party. Try using different voices for different characters. And speak slowly. To further frighten your intended creepfest victims, turn out the lights and use a flashlight to create an eerie mood. BOO!

7. Know all the words by heart to your favorite songs.

For sing-a-long perfection, grab your fave CD, take the cover out of the plastic holder, and see if the lyrics have been printed inside. If so, make yourself comfy, hit "play," and read along as the singer sings. If the words aren't printed inside, listen to the songs and try to write down the words as you listen. And—please!—remember your family's sanity if learning lyrics means you'll be playing the same song 42 times in a row. Thanks!

8. Learn where the free stuff is at the mall.

Sure, the folks at Sausage World are generous in offering meat-on-a-toothpick hors d'oeuvres. But did you know department store cosmetics counters have sample perfumes and lipsticks? Just walk up to a salesgirl who's not busy with a customer and say, "I'd like some sample products and your business card because I'm planning to buy enough for a new look this year." Then get a makeover for free, and see how you look and feel.

9. Have fewer fights with your friends.

It happens to everyone. One day everything's cool; the next day all your friends are ticked off at you—and you don't even know why. How to avoid this? Treat other people as you want to be treated. If you think you've irked a pal, tell her you're sorry and promise to be more careful of her feelings. If a friend does something to peeve you, tell her nicely why it gets under your skin, and then forgive her. Remember, giving her the silent treatment is the worst thing to do.

10. Have less stressful mornings.

Does it feel like roosters sleep later than you do? Well, sorry, Charlie, but the only way to mellow your mornings is to get up earlier. Try these tips: Set your clock five minutes fast, and then program the alarm to go off 15 minutes earlier. Place the clock on a dresser across the room so you have to get out of bed to turn it off. Have your clothes picked out the night before, and have your backpack all ready to go. Think of how chaotic your mornings used to be, as you leisurely enjoy some cocoa while waiting for the bus.

11. Win more contests.

Winning stuff is better than an easy A. To win giveaways in magazines, the trick is to send in the entry form as soon as you read about the contest, because the number of  prizes is always limited. And one other note: Follow the directions. Says one contest judge, "It sounds brutal, but we've had to toss more than a few entries into the trash because girls didn't completely fill out the entry forms." So be a big winner, and fill in those blanks!

12. Be the block's best baby-sitter.

We found one universal rule when it comes to successful baby-sitting: Play with the kids! "Some girls see baby-sitting as a night of TV and talking on the phone to their friends," says Laura, who plans to start baby-sitting in a year or two. "If a sitter ignored me, I would tell my mom not to call her again. A baby-sitter should care about what the kids are doing."

No callback equals no more baby-sitting money. Think about it.

13. Handle a diss better.

If a mean boy calls you "Fishface," do you go home and examine your mug in the mirror to look for gills? Well, stop that right now—because it's very important that you don't believe for two seconds the harsh things other people say about you. Of course, that's not so easy when the diss is true. What do you do when the class know-it-all feels the need to publicly point out the D you just got on the pop quiz? Just cool the confrontation. Say, "Thank you. How kind of you to notice." Then, whatever you do, change the subject! Whew!

14. Be less afraid of... the dark, bugs, etc....

When you're super-afraid of something and don't know why, it's called a phobia. Whether you're bug-phobic or homework-phobic (ha-ha), you can help yourself. First, make a mantra (a sentence you say in your head over and over again) that you can repeat to yourself when you're feeling scared: "There is nobody under my bed!" or, "I can crush that ugly bug!" Mentally repeating a mantra won't make your fears go away, but it *will* help calm you down. Then, squish that bug and show it who's boss!

15. Read more books.

Reading exercises your brain muscles and makes you smarter. It also makes you more attuned to the world because you share the thoughts, emotions and experiences of countless characters. But we understand that it's hard to squeeze non-school books into your busy schedule. Even if it's for only a few minutes, like in line at lunch, on the bus, or whenever you have some down time, read a lightweight paperback just for fun.

16. Be less nervous about ordering in restaurants.

Sometimes waiters or waitresses are scary, and that goes double for glamorous hair stylists, snooty salespeople, and other adults who treat kids like brainless babies. You can deal by putting on your best actress airs: Suck in a deep breath, hold your chin up high, and clearly and audibly tell the person what you want. The thing to remember is that they really are there to serve you, but they can't do that if you don't speak up.

17. Write a better letter to your friends.

Do you like passing notes?
__Yes
__No
We guess yes, so here are a few tips: For handwritten notes, tear out a cool picture from a magazine (like a fashion photo) and write directly on the picture with markers for a look that's way better than plain binder paper. For cool e-mails, write about all your favorite topics, but write it like a multiple-choice quiz so your friend is part of the letter and not just sitting and reading. And be sure not to make every question yes/no. Try this: What's your favorite mag?
__*Girls' Life*
__*Auto Life*
__*Bug Life*
We wonder....

18. Decorate your room way cooler...for free.

Is your room a shrine to everything you loved in first grade? Begin by making your room reflect more of who you are now. Start by packing away the toys you don't play with anymore. Next, display snapshots of you and friends in the crease of a dresser mirror, on the nightstand, and in collage frames on the walls. Another decor tip: Tear out pictures you like from magazines (trim the jagged edges) and tape them on a wall in a cool collage. And don't overlook yard sales. Sure, that wood dresser is ugly, but just about anything looks great after a few coats of paint. Then, pick some flowers for your nightstand. How domestic.

19. Keep a secret longer.

Keeping a secret can be like holding a sneeze in a pepper factory. If you can't stand it, write the secret in your journal so you feel like you're telling *someone*. If telling the secret will bum out a friend, you need reminders of that. Put on a ring you can wear on several different fingers—it'll feel funny and every time you look at it, you'll remember to keep your lips zipped. If the secret's about you, keep it from school gossips by confiding in an aunt or friend who lives far away. Sssshhhh....

20. Triumph at try-outs.

What does it take to make the cut? It takes effort. But there's more to it than that. You don't have to be the best. Coaches are always looking for desire, enthusiasm, and potential—in addition to talent. One high school swim coach admits his favorite team member isn't a very strong swimmer. "But she's got the best attitude, which is vital to our team spirit," he says.

21. Ace a test.

Sitting down to a test and going blank stinks. Knowing you're about as prepared for the test as you are for an alien invasion is even worse. Take neat and detailed notes during class. When you get home, take 20 minutes to read over your notes and highlight the most important stuff. If you keep up with what's going on in class every day, cramming will be a thing of the past. The night before the big exam, you should only need to review the important stuff. If you have time in the morning, go over your notes again to remind yourself, "Hey, I know this stuff!" When taking the actual exam, answer the questions you know first, and go back to the ones you have to think about. Once you're finished, check over the exam to make sure you didn't skip a question. Hand that sucker in, and go celebrate your A!

22. Cure weekend boredom.

Once you're bored, it's almost impossible to think of exciting stuff to keep you busy. So figure out what to do with yourself before you become bored out of your gourd. Start a to-do list, and tuck it away in a desk drawer or post it on your bulletin board. You'll have it handy next time a boring weekend rolls around. Hey, it sure beats watching endless reruns.

23. Get elected class president.

It doesn't matter who you're up against—you *can* sweep the school election. Honor students, homecoming queens, and teachers' pets don't stand a chance if you follow these suggestions. Be genuinely friendly and outgoing. Winning candidates talk to everyone who votes—not just their friends or the popular people. You'd be surprised how many kids don't vote—reach out to them and convince them to cast one in your favor. And you need name recognition, so hang a few posters around school featuring your name in big, bold letters. Hand out small buttons and some candy with your name on it. Last, give a short-and-sweet speech. Talk about specific things you'll work to change, like the nasty meatloaf sandwiches in the school caf, instead of making broad promises.

24. Tell a joke.

Everyone loves a natural cut-up. Your humorous side is like a muscle—the more you use it, the stronger it gets. Just wait for a pause in a conversation that reminds you of one of your jokes, and then launch right into it. Don't ever force a joke because then there's extra pressure for it to be funny. And have no fear if you fumble through it—your mistakes will add to the humor. Just make sure you follow the golden rule: Don't start a joke unless, in fact, you do know the ending. Still need practice? Hang around funny people, and lift a few of their best lines.

25. Wriggle out of embarrassment.

Whoops! You slip and there go your chili-cheese nachos—all over the cashier in the lunch line. Everyone is snickering, and all you want to do is disappear into the guacamole vat. You could either slither away into goofball obscurity...or you could make the most of your mishap. Embrace the moment. Act like you just finished a gold-grabbing gymnastics routine. Put your arms in the air and say, "That deserves a 10!" The key is to always own up to your goof and make light of it—that takes the pressure off. Same if you say something silly— own the mistake. Say, "Wait, did I say that? Let me rewind. I meant to say, [insert correct phrase here]." Keep talking, and your slip-up should slip people's minds.

26. Get good deals at the mall.

There's no reason you have to help huge bajillionaire companies fatten up their bank accounts. Instead, plump up your own piggie by saving beaucoup bucks. Words to live by: Never pay full price! All stores mark down goodies regularly to make room for new stuff that arrives. If you're serious about saving, stick to the sales racks. Be patient. Full-price clothes usually wind up on sale within a few months. Find out when your fave stores do markdowns. Most chains have a specific day-of-the-week or a particular month devoted to price-slashing. Plus, there are always great end-of-season sales. Bargain shop your booty off, and you'll end up with more dough stashed in your cargo pockets.

27. Remember more.

Your keys, homework, wallet, concert tickets, lip gloss—just a few of the things on your Most Likely To Get Lost list. Ever wish you could super-charge your memory? Whenever you can't find or remember something, it's because you weren't aware of it in the first place. Put simply, you are doing things absentmindedly. Try this: Next time you lay down your keys, be aware of your action, then imagine the key crashing to the ground. Add a surprising visual to everything you do—from putting away items to memorizing facts—and you'll be twice as likely to recall stuff later.

28. Tell your crush you like him.

First things first. Get to know him and make sure he really is as cool as you think he is. Hang around him, talk to him in class and get to know his friends. If you still deem him worthy, go for it. Wait until he is alone, and ask him over to study. Keep it short and sweet. A simple invitation says it all. If you're the shy type, write him a short note. Then comes the hard part—waiting to see how he'll respond. Don't call him or bug him because that will make him

uncomfortable. If the guy balks or makes a million excuses, move on—fast. While he might like you, he might not *like you* like you. But if he jumps on your invite, chances are good that he has a crush on you, too.

29. Fit in with a new group of friends.

Whether you're the new girl or just expanding your friendship circle, it's hard to mesh with a new crew. But even without psychic mind-scanning abilities, you can still scope out new buds pretty easily. Life's too short for bad friends! But if a particular group makes you feel welcome, invite them to your house, share little secrets and offer to host a study group. But remember—your new friends, if they are true pals, aren't hanging with you because of your clothes or other silly superficial reasons. They like you for you.

30. Read aloud in class.

Why does it feel like a public flogging every time you have to speak in class? Usually, it's just a serious case of self-consciousness. Here's how to ease read-out-loud anxiety attacks. Start by reading aloud at home. Yes, you might feel a little silly reciting Shakespeare to your goldfish, but the idea is to get comfortable with hearing yourself recite. Then the next time you're in class and get called on, imagine it's just you and Goldie, and get on with it. Be sure to breathe in and out—many people unconsciously hold their breath when they're nervous! And take your time—you're not in a speed-reading contest. The more you rush, the more you'll mess up.

31. Make someone's day.

Why not do something nice for a friend, family member or, heck, even a long-lost cousin's boyfriend's next-door neighbor? Spread a little love! Just think how great you feel when someone does something unexpectedly sweet for you. You don't have to throw someone a no-holds-barred birthday bash or buy your sis an expensive gift to show you care. Instead, tell your friend she's a great listener or wash the dishes for your mom without being asked. Help an elderly lady with her grocery bags, or offer to baby-sit your neighbor's toddlers —for free. If you're having a lousy afternoon, this kind of stuff can work wonders for lifting a mood.

Keep Smiling!

Is your future already looking a little brighter? That's because you shine like a star! (Girl, you're blinding us.) By now, you should be feeling pretty great about being you. And once you can bask in your own personal spotlight, all the people around you should notice that special spark, too. Just what can you do with that spark? Well, the possibilities are endless.

But your overall success depends on you—and bringing out the best in yourself. How well you do in school, how you handle sticky situations, even how you carry yourself in that bathing suit are all linked to your self-esteem.

Don't let it slip. Keep that killer new confidence in check with daily reminders of how awesome you are. Stay on track, and never turn your back on the most important person in your life. *You*!

Credits

When we first had the idea for *The GL Guide to Being the Best You*, we didn't have a clue what we were getting into. After putting out *GL* for nine years, we had so much great self-esteem advice to share with you, we hardly knew how to pack it all in. But, what you are holding in your hands is the best of the best.

We would like to give major thanks to those whose talents made this book and who make *GL* magazine great. As they say, behind every great magazine is a super talented team of editors, writers, and designers. And for the past nine years, *GL* has been lucky enough to have some of the best. Thanks a million to executive editor Kelly White, Chun Kim, Sarah Cordi, Georgia Wilson, and Debbie Chaillou. And thanks, too, to the great folks at Scholastic. We could never have done this book without you.

Writing Credits

Chapter 1: *The Big E!* (Roni Cohen-Sandler), *Be Your Own Cheerleading Squad* (Jodi Lynn Bryson), *Up Your Confidence Quotient* (Robin Baade), *Being True to You!* (Michelle Silver), *Quiz: Assert Yourself!* (Roni Cohen-Sandler)

Chapter 2: *Mind Over Body* (Karen Bokram), *Six Secrets to a Killer Body Image* (Karen Bokram), *Take My Body Type, Please* (Roni Cohen-Sandler), *Quiz: Weigh Your Body Confidence* (Michelle Silver)

Chapter 3: *The Secrets to School Success* (Roni Cohen-Sandler), *Teachers 101* (Roni Cohen-Sandler), *Score Big Time with Your Teachers* (Raquel Singer Klein), *This is Only a Test* (Michelle Silver), *How to Deal with Tricky School Sitches* (Michelle Silver), *Ouch! That Hurts* (Kelly White)

Chapter 4: *Miss Perfect—Not!* (Roni Cohen-Sandler), *To Lie or Not to Lie* (Roni Cohen-Sandler), *Rumor Mill Central* (Roni Cohen-Sandler), *Quiz: Groovy Gossip Gauge* (Lisa Mulcahy), *Help! When Everyday Sitches Get Sticky* (Taylor Morris)

Chapter 5: *Go for Gutsy* (Lisa Mulcahy), *Quiz: Are You Game?* (Audrey Brashich), *Say Goodbye to Being Shy* (Anne Vassal), *Shake Those Labels!* (Roni Cohen-Sandler), *Quiz: Face to Face with Fear!* (Lisa Mulcahy), *31 Things You Can Do Better* (Kristen Kemp and Jodi Lynn Bryson)